SpringerBriefs in Law

SpringerBriefs present concise summaries of cutting-edge research and practical applications across a wide spectrum of fields. Featuring compact volumes of 50 to 125 pages, the series covers a range of content from professional to academic. Typical topics might include:

- A timely report of state-of-the art analytical techniques
- A bridge between new research results, as published in journal articles, and a contextual literature review
- A snapshot of a hot or emerging topic
- A presentation of core concepts that students must understand in order to make independent contributions

SpringerBriefs in Law showcase emerging theory, empirical research, and practical application in Law from a global author community. SpringerBriefs are characterized by fast, global electronic dissemination, standard publishing contracts, standardized manuscript preparation and formatting guidelines, and expedited production schedules.

Dominik Zając

Non-state Actors Law-making and Domestic Criminal Law

Springer

Dominik Zając
Department of Criminal Law
Jagiellonian University
Kraków, Poland

ISSN 2192-855X ISSN 2192-8568 (electronic)
SpringerBriefs in Law
ISBN 978-3-031-47869-7 ISBN 978-3-031-47870-3 (eBook)
https://doi.org/10.1007/978-3-031-47870-3

This publication has been produced as part of the Bekker Scholarship, funded by the Polish National Agency for Academic Exchange, project number: BPN/BEK/2021/2/00003/U/00001.

This Springer imprint is published by the registered company Springer Nature Switzerland AG
The registered company address is: Gewerbestrasse 11, 6330 Cham, Switzerland

Paper in this product is recyclable.

Contents

Abbreviations

CE	Council of Europe
CSR	Corporate Social Responsibility
ECHR	European Convention of Human Rights
ECtHR	European Court of Human Rights
EEA	European Economic Area
EU	European Union
GHTF	Global Harmonization Task Force
HRC	Human Rights Committee
ICANN	Internet Corporation for Assigned Names and Numbers
ICAO	International Civil Aviation Organization
ICC	International Criminal Court
ICJ	International Court of Justice
ICL	International Criminal Law
ICRC	International Committee of the Red Cross
ICTR	International Criminal Tribunal for Rwanda
ICTY	International Criminal Tribunal for the Former Yugoslavia
INGO	International Non-governmental Organization
ISO	International Organization for Standardization
MNE	Multinational Enterprise
OECD	Organisation for Economic Cooperation and Development
PCIJ	Permanent Court of International Justice
TFEU	Treaty on the Functioning of the European Union
UNTS	United Nations Treaty Series

Chapter 1
Introduction

Abstract Domestic criminal law is increasingly influenced by broader international law. The latter, in turn, is multicentric in nature, increasingly created by non-state actors. This book attempts to characterise the impact of statements formulated by non-state actors on the content of national penal norms as applied by criminal courts.

Keywords Non-state actors · Criminal law · International law · Penal norms

In a globalised world, international law-making is playing an increasingly important role. International law is no longer merely an instrument for regulating international relations. It binds directly individuals or state officials. This poses a serious challenge for those responsible for applying the law.[1] National courts, including criminal courts,[2] have to face the problem of incorporating these into the norm they interpret.

The above process also involves non-state actors. The regulations they formulate impinge on the legal situation of other subjects of international law as well as individuals. The legislative activities of the UN Security Council, the organs of the European Union, and finally organisations such as the International Olympic Committee determine not only the conducts of states, but also of their citizens.

This study attempts to systematise the legal reasoning that should be carried out by the domestic criminal court—in order to include the regulations[3] formulated by non-state actors, into the domestic penal norms. Their content influences the shape of the premises for criminal liability. However, this influence is not uniform in nature. It depends on the type of non-state actor, the source of competence to make law, and finally on the content of the formulated regulation.

Further considerations are divided into eight chapters.

The first contains introduction.

The second chapter characterises the process of making criminal law regulations as one aspect of the exercise of *ius puniendi.* The third one presents a normative

[1] Österdahl (2015, p. 134).

[2] Satzger (2017, p. 1).

[3] The terms "regulations" and "elements of norms" are used interchangeably in this work to denote those statements of law-makers that can be included as elements of penal norms.

D. Zając, *Non-state Actors Law-making and Domestic Criminal Law*,
SpringerBriefs in Law, https://doi.org/10.1007/978-3-031-47870-3_1

approach to the criteria of imputation of criminal responsibility, referring to two categories of penal norms: those that bind the individual and those that bind the court. The fourth chapter contains an analysis of the group of non-state actors as law-makers, taking into account the source of the power to legislate. The fifth chapter presents a typology of regulations formulated by non-state actors, taking as criteria for division those features that are crucial for determining the influence they exert on the shape of national criminal law. The sixth chapter contains considerations on how to eliminate conflicts that may arise between different regulations of non-state actors competing for inclusion in the content of the penal norm.

The seventh chapter of the study contains a description of the method of incorporating regulations formulated by non-state actors into the content of penal norms. In it, I refer to the findings made in earlier sections of the work. It provides a synthetic description of the judicial inference that should be carried out when determining the criteria for criminal responsibility and the sentence—taking into account the legislative activity of non-state actors.

The eighth chapter contains conclusions.

This publication has been produced as part of the Bekker Scholarship, funded by the Polish National Agency for Academic Exchange, project number: BPN/BEK/2021/2/00003/U/00001. I would like to give special thanks to Prof. Kai Ambos, for giving me the opportunity to conduct research at the University of Göttingen, and to Prof. Petr Rackow, for his insightful comments on the text. Thanks are also due to my colleagues at the Department of Criminal Law at Jagiellonian University, who subjected my work to critical analysis during the Department's seminar.

References

Österdahl I (2015) (International) Law! In: Liivoja R, Petman J (eds) International law-making: essays in honour of Jan Klabbers, 1st edn. Routledge, Abingdon, Oxon

Satzger H (2017) International and European criminal law, 2nd edn. C.H. Beck, München, Germany; Oxford, United Kingdom; Baden-Baden, Germany

Chapter 2
The Making of Criminal Law as an Element of *Ius Puniendi*

Abstract The creation of criminal law regulations is part of the exercise of *ius puniendi*, which in turn is considered to be an exclusive competence of the state. At the same time, however, law-making is increasingly conditioned by the content of international law. This chapter presents possible points of interference by the statements of international non-state actors on the content of domestic criminal law.

Keywords *Ius puniendi* · *Domaine réservé* · Criminal law · Non-state actors

2.1 Introduction

Ius puniendi is the competence of the state that allows punishing an individual for socially harmful behaviour.[1] Traditionally, it is an element of power belonging to both imperium and *domaine réservé*.[2] The inclusion of the *ius puniendi* among the competences belonging to the imperium means that only entities with this type of power can exercise the right of punishment. The classification of the *ius puniendi* among the powers belonging to the imperium means that only entities possessing this type of power can exercise the right of punishment. The inclusion within the scope of the *domaine réservé* gives this power an exclusive character—no other entity, not even those possessing the imperium, can interfere with the way in which the right of punishment is exercised by the holder (a particular state).

States have the primary entitlement to impose punishment in the majesty of the law. Other entities may exercise *ius puniendi* only by delegation.[3] The above situation is not the simple result of historical events. It is a consequence of accepting the idea of imperium as a power requiring a special legitimacy, belonging only to states. One

[1] On the conception of criminal law see inter alia: Duff and Green (2011, p. 127), Ambos (2021, p. 101), Klip (2021, p. 239), Fletcher (1998, p. 10), Dubber and Hörnle (2016), Heinze and Fyfe (2018, p. 14), Green (1990, p. 134). As Heinze and Fyfe indicate: "*ius puniendi* is the State power to punish, that is, the State's capacity—resulting from its sovereignty—to declare certain conduct as punishable and to determine a sentence".

[2] Ambos (2013, p. 311), Satzger (2017, p. 1).

[3] Ambos (2021, p. 101), Ambos (2013, p. 298), Pavel (2014, p. 36), Heinze and Fyfe (2018, p. 17).

D. Zając, *Non-state Actors Law-making and Domestic Criminal Law*, SpringerBriefs in Law, https://doi.org/10.1007/978-3-031-47870-3_2

of its elements is the right to use coercion,[4] and the exercise of the *ius puniendi* is one of the most drastic of its forms.

Ius puniendi is not homogeneous. It comprises both the power to make law (legislative jurisdiction/legislative power) and the power to enforce it in a process (judicial jurisdiction/judiciary power).[5] By exercising the *ius puniendi*, the state imposes a penalty on a specific person, but also specifies the premises for its imposition. In such categories one should perceive the formulation of the provisions of substantive criminal law, which define the criteria for the application of coercion of state. Regulations of this type are not consensual and do not bind by the will of the parties, but constitute the basis for the sovereign actions of the state, independent of the consent of the individual.

Establishing regulations in the field of criminal law is therefore an element of the exercise of the *ius puniendi.*[6] There are significant consequences from the above.

The criteria for assigning criminal liability cannot be determined by an entity that lacks the legitimacy to exercise an imperium. The state derives such legitimacy directly from sovereignty.[7] The state is also the only entity whose task is to create a comprehensive legal system that guarantees the stable development of the public sphere, taking into account the interests of society as a whole.[8] The manner of conduct of states it this field may not be regulated by any superior legislator. There is no entity that would exercise power over them. It is confirmed, inter alia, in the wording of Art. 2 Charter of the UN.[9]

Therefore, the possibility of formulating regulations of penal character by non-state actors is significantly limited. As a general rule, entities of this type do not have the authority required to exercise this type of legislation. Because of that fact, unlike other branches of law, such as trade[10] or aviation law,[11] criminal law is not

---

[4] Green (1990, p. 71), Morris (2012), Heinze and Fyfe (2018, p. 16).

[5] Ambos (2021, p. 101), Heinze and Fyfe (2018).

[6] Robert (2020, p. 5), Heinze and Fyfe (2018, p. 16).

[7] Brolmann and Radi (2016, p. 13), Benvenisti (2015, p. 5); S.S. "Lotus", France v Turkey, Judgment, Judgment No 9, PCIJ Series A No 10, ICGJ 248 (PCIJ 1927), (1935) 2 Hudson, World Ct Rep 20, 7th September 1927, https://www.icj-cij.org/public/files/permanent-court-of-international-justice/serie_A/A_10/30_Lotus_Arret.pdf. The judgment indicated: "International law governs relations between independent States. The rules of law binding upon States therefore emanate from their own free will as expressed in conventions or by usages generally accepted as expressing principles of law and established in order to regulate the relations between these co-existing independent communities or with a view to the achievement of common aims. Restrictions upon the independence of States cannot therefore be presumed".

[8] Palombella (2015, p. 71).

[9] Charter of the United Nations, 24 October 1945, 1 UNTS XVI, https://treaties.un.org/doc/publication/ctc/uncharter.pdf. The Article 1 (1) of the Charter states: "The Organization is based on the principle of the sovereign equality of all its Members".

[10] In this field see: Marrakesh Agreement Establishing the World Trade Organization, Apr. 15, 1994, 1867 UNTS 154, 33 I.L.M. 1144 (1994), https://treaties.un.org/doc/Publication/UNTS/Volume%201867/volume-1867-A-31874-English.pdf; Srivastava (2020).

[11] The legislative activity of the International Civil Aviation Organisation (ICAO) is of particular importance; see: International Civil Aviation Organization (ICAO), Convention on Civil Aviation

the subject of direct interest to non-state actors. Moreover, penal regulations should remain outside the influence of external factors, as a result of the legislative process remaining in the *domaine réservé*.

In practice, international law influences the way in which this competence is exercised. There are three aspects of such impact.

First of all, criminal law is not a closed system, but makes more and more use of references.[12] It penalises violations of regulations contained in non-penal acts. Regulations referred to in criminal law do not have to deal with issues pertaining to the *domaine réservé* or imperium.

Second, the competence to perform the *ius puniendi* as an element of the *domaine réservé* is seen primarily as a right of positive character. In this approach, the state has the exclusive power to recognise that a given behaviour should constitute a crime. Apart from exceptions (grave breaches of human rights[13]), international law cannot require penalization an individual's behaviour, without consent of states. At the same time, at the international level, the state's ability to criminalise is very often limited due to the need to respect human rights.[14] To put it simply: only the state can criminalise a given act, but not in every case making such a decision will be permissible from the perspective of international law. The source of the above asymmetry is the increasingly stronger position of the human rights protection system, limiting the freedom of state action in contact with an individual. The classic principle of *nullum crimen sine lege*[15] is supplemented with a number of additional restrictions, also relating to substantive criminal law.[16]

Third, states do not act in a vacuum in their legislative activity. They are bound by international obligations and declare their willingness to shape internal practices in a specific way. In this respect, the state remains the decisive entity, albeit in agreement with the other signatories. The shape of *ius puniendi* is influenced also by regulations formulated by non-state actors, which increasingly determine the legal situation of not only states but also individuals or state officials.

The aim of this study is to determine the impact of the legislative activity of non-state actors on the criteria of criminal liability. Let us therefore turn to the characterisation of the criteria for assigning responsibility themselves. They will then serve as a point of reference in further analyses, directly related to the law-making activity of non-state actors. It is impossible to talk about the impact itself without knowing what the impact is about.

("Chicago Convention"), 7 December 1944, (1994) 15 UNTS 295, https://www.icao.int/publications/Documents/7300_orig.pdf; Bartsch (2018, p. 156). Autor indicates: "ICAO with respect to aircraft accident investigation is such that the investigation of accidents should not be the basis—or even the source—of a prosecution action against aviation personel".

[12] Satzger (2017, pp. 3, 101).

[13] Ambos (2021, p. 100), Satzger (2017, p. 2), Heinze and Fyfe (2018, p. 18).

[14] Ambos (2021, p. 100), Pavel (2014, p. 36), Heinze and Fyfe (2018, p. 19).

[15] Peristeridou (2011, p. 69).

[16] Klip (2021, p. 245).

References

Ambos K (2013) Punishment without a Sovereign? The ius puniendi issue of international criminal law: a first contribution towards a consistent theory of international criminal law. Oxf J Leg Stud 33:293–315

Ambos K (2021) Treatise on international criminal law, vol I: foundations and general part, 2nd edn. Oxford University Press, Oxford, New York

Bartsch R (2018) International aviation law, 2nd edn. Routledge, London, New York

Benvenisti E (2015) Legislating for humanity. In: Liivoja R, Petman J (eds) International law-making: essays in honour of Jan Klabbers, 1st edn. Routledge, Abingdon, Oxon

Brolmann C, Radi Y (2016) Research handbook on the theory and practice of international lawmaking. Edward Elgar Publishing, Cheltenham, UK Northhampton, MA, USA

Dubber MD, Hörnle T (2016) The Oxford handbook of criminal law, Reprint. Oxford University Press, Oxford

Duff RA, Green S (2011) Philosophical foundations of criminal law, 1st edn. Oxford University Press, Oxford, New York

Fletcher GP (1998) Basic concepts of criminal law. Oxford University Press, New York

Green L (1990) The authority of the state. Oxford University Press, Oxford, New York

Heinze A, Fyfe S (2018) The normative framework of preliminary examinations. In: Bergsmo M, Stahn C (eds) Quality control in preliminary examination, vol 2. Torkel Opsahl Academic, Brussels

Klip A (2021) European criminal law: an integrative approach, 4th edn. Intersentia, Cambridge Antwerp Chicago

Morris CW (2012) State coercion and force. Soc Philos Policy 29:28–49. https://doi.org/10.1017/S0265052511000094

Palombella G (2015) Global legislation and its discontents. In: Liivoja R, Petman J (eds) International law-making: essays in honour of Jan Klabbers, 1st edn. Routledge, Abingdon, Oxon

Pavel C (2014) Divided sovereignty: international institutions and the limits of state authority. Oxford University Press, Oxford, New York

Peristeridou C (2011) The principle of lex certa in national law and European perspectives. In: Klip A (ed) Substantive criminal law of the European Union. Maklu, Antwerpen

Robert C (2020) Theories of punishment. In: Focquaert F, Shaw E, Waller BN (eds) The Routledge handbook of the philosophy and science of punishment, 1st edn. Routledge, New York, NY; Milton Park, Abingdon, Oxon

Satzger H (2017) International and European criminal law, 2nd edn. C.H. Beck, München, Oxford, Baden-Baden

Srivastava A (2020) Modern law of international trade: comparative export trade and international harmonization, 1st edn, 2020 edn. Springer, Singapore

Chapter 3
Substantive Criminal Law in the Normative Approach

Abstract Criminal law describes the criteria for holding an offender criminally responsible. Such criteria, when interpreted in a specific case, should form an unambiguous, coherent and clear directive of conduct—penal norm. This chapter describes the underlying assumptions of the normative view of criminal law, explaining the concept of penal norms. In doing so, it provides a theoretical foundation for further considerations.

Keywords Penal norms · The primary norm · Verhaltensnorm · The secondary norm · Sanktionsnorm · Elements of norm

Criteria of criminal liability are defined by substantive criminal law.[1] It consists of a complex set of provisions, also of a reference nature. Their combined use allows to establish the premises of criminal liability binding in concrete case and the imposition of a penalty on perpetrator. For example: to punish someone for causing a fatal road accident it is necessary, among others showing that he violated the road traffic regulations and that it was this breach that resulted in the criminal result (death). Putting the above circumstances into a systematic model supporting the reasoning of court (state officials) is not a trivial matter. In the theory of criminal law, this issue is approached in various ways. Some dogmatists refer to the concept of the structure of a crime, distinguishing the plane of punishability, unlawfulness and culpability.[2] Others refer to elements of the crime, supplemented by general rules.[3] From the perspective of this study, the normative approach seems to be the most adequate tool.[4] It describes the criteria of criminal liability through the prism of relations between regulations binding addressee (elements of norms), regardless of the entities that established them. The normative approach allows the broadest scope

---

[1] On substantive criminal law see inter alia: Kratochwil (1989, p. 186), Fletcher (1998, pp. 7–14), Satzger (2017), Fletcher (2000), Duff and Green (2011).

[2] Fletcher (2000, p. 406).

[3] Ibid., p. 406; Weaver et al. (2021, p. 63).

[4] On norms see inter alia: Paulson (1988), Kratochwil (1989), Alchourron and Bulygin (1971), Atienza and Manero (1998), Wright (1963), Kelsen (1957).

D. Zając, *Non-state Actors Law-making and Domestic Criminal Law*,
SpringerBriefs in Law, https://doi.org/10.1007/978-3-031-47870-3_3

to capture the diversity of these elements and their mutual relations. This, in turn, allows for a systematic analysis of the premises of criminal liability, also taking into account regulations formulated by non-state actors.

3.1 Basic Assumptions of the Normative Method

The normative method is based on the following assumptions.[5]

First, the focal point is the norm, understood as a coherent directive of conduct, binding the addressee[6] in a given situation, constructed on the basis of many normative statements (provisions of law, rules of art, previous judicial decision, etc.).[7] In theoretical terms, it consists of two elements: a hypothesis and a disposition.[8] The hypothesis describes the circumstances in which the addressee found himself, the disposition indicates the desired behaviour (if X finds himself in the situation Y, he should act in the manner Z). Referring to the above-mentioned perpetrator of the road accident: the hypothesis of the binding norm would refer to his driving a vehicle in land traffic, while the instruction would indicate certain rules of road traffic, described in detail in the law. Both the hypothesis and the disposition of the norm are established by taking into account all regulations that bind him in a given context, at the moment of the addressee's behaviour. A norm formulates a prohibition or obligation to act and must be cognisable at the time of the action/omission of the subject it binds. Only in this way will it be possible to ensure the fundamental purpose of the law, which is to regulate human behaviour and to respond to its violation.[9]

Secondly, norms consist of many elements. But it is the norm, and not its constituent elements, that has the value of being binding. It is the norm, as a certain result of the interpretation of the law, that binds the addressee. In the proposed approach, the individual regulations formulated by the legislative actors (states, but also non-state actors) are characterised by their normative capacity. These regulations may or may not become a constituent element of the norm in a given situation.

Thirdly, in the case of criminal law, two addressees of norms can be distinguished.[10] On the one hand, the norms of substantive criminal law are addressed to the individual as a subject to criminal liability. In this regard, they indicate how an individual should behave in order not to be punished. On the other hand, the

[5] The considerations presented here do not constitute a comprehensive discussion of the concept of norm in legal theory. Rather, they are an attempt at a simplified adaptation of their underlying assumptions for the purposes of criminal law interpretation. Such an approach is developed among Polish criminal law theorists and dogmatists. See inter alia: Kardas (2011, 2012), Dąbrowska-Kardas (2012), Wróbel (2003), Pohl (2007), Zoll (1990), Ziembiński (1960).

[6] Paulson (1988, p. 62).

[7] Ibid., p. 59.

[8] Simplification is used here; legal theory distinguishes more elements of a norm, but the two indicated are crucial for further discussion. See also: Wright (1963, p. 70).

[9] Rostalski (2019, p. 20).

[10] Kelsen (1957, pp. 274–275), Hallevy (2010, p. 16), Paulson (1988, p. 66).

addressees of the norms of criminal law are also state authorities, which are obliged to impose a penalty for breaking the law (court).[11] Here, penal norms also regulate the subject's behaviour, however, they refer to taking certain conventional actions. They indicate what circumstances should be taken into account in order to recognise an individual as the perpetrator of a crime and impose a penalty on him.

Both the purpose and the moment of establishing the content of the norms addressed to the two distinguished categories of subjects are different. Its purpose is to show the individual how to behave in a given situation in order not to be punished.[12] In the case of individual, the norm refers to circumstances that already exist at the time of his act/omission. The court evaluates the perpetrator's act ex post. Thus, it may take into account aspects of the event which are of a follow-up nature, e.g. the number of victims who died as a result of the perpetrator's act. Here, the purpose of the norm is to define the premises and method of punishing an individual who violates the law. Therefore, two categories of penal norms that are not identical in terms of content should be distinguished: the norm of individual and the norm of court (state official).

Both categories of norms are related in terms of content and function. One of the conditions for the imposition of a penalty against the perpetrator of the crime (norm of court) is proving that his behaviour violated the norm that bound him for the moment of act (norm of individual). Without violating the norm of the individual, the disposition of the norm of the court will not be triggered. Both norms are interconnected—coupled (coupling theory[13]). However, both types of norms have a different structure and are decoded in a slightly different way. The key question is to what extent they can be shaped by non-state actors' law-making activity. For this purpose, it is necessary to present an in-depth theoretical analysis relating to their structure.

Relating the above to the classical theory of norms, it can be pointed out that a norm binding on an individual corresponds in principle to the primary norm (Verhaltensnorm),[14] while a norm binding on an authority corresponds to the secondary norm (Sanktionsnorm).[15] However, taking into account the specific context of *ius puniendi*, as well as the peculiar construction of the norms in question outlined below, I have decided to abandon the accepted nomenclature, for the sake of clarity of the argument, and adopt descriptive names. This is supported by two circumstances. Firstly, the concepts of Kelsen,[16] Bulygin,[17] Manero and Atienza,[18] Raz[19] or Hart,[20]

---

[11] Paulson (1988, p. 62).

[12] See also: Alchourron and Bulygin (1971, p. 42).

[13] Paulson (1988, p. 64), Kelsen (1957, p. 275).

[14] Atienza and Manero (1998, p. 14), Rostalski (2019, p. 17), Aichele et al. (2022).

[15] Atienza and Manero (1998, p. 12), Alchourron and Bulygin (1971, p. 151), Rostalski (2019, p. 17).

[16] Kelsen (1971).

[17] Alchourron and Bulygin (1971).

[18] Atienza and Manero (1998).

[19] Raz (1980).

[20] Hart et al. (2012).

as well as those of the Poznan theorists[21] differ in detail, broadening the perspective on the norm of law. None of these, however, is a dedicated tool for conducting a criminal law analysis. The approach presented below corresponds most closely to Alchourron and Bulygin's approach of constructing a case-specific norm (in German legal theory, to Rostalski's concept).[22] Secondly, such a state of affairs requires the presentation of a construction of the norm that would take into account the specificity of penal norms. Introducing such criteria and at the same time retaining the nomenclature does not lead to a simplification or clarification of the argument, but is misleading. At the same time, for the purposes of judicial inference, maintaining such a profound theoretical coherence as presented by the concepts of Alchourron and Bulygin is not necessary. The concept of norm served here as a tool in the process of interpretation of the law and not as an object of inquiry.

3.2 The Norm of an Individual

The central element of the norm of individual is the prohibition/order of conduct, connected with the threat of imposition of punishment on individual, who breaks it. It is derived from the penalising provision. In the proposed approach, it is the starting point to which other regulations refer. The content of the prohibition/order is then further clarified in the interpretation process by taking into account the content of other normative statements relating to the individual's behaviour.

Let us consider the above using the example of the aforementioned situation of causing a car accident. Most jurisdictions have provisions that penalise this type of behaviour. According to § 229 of the German Penal Code: "Whoever causes bodily harm to another by negligence incurs a penalty of imprisonment for a term not exceeding three years or a fine".[23] In turn, the Road Traffic Act 1988, Section 1A states: "(1) A person who causes serious injury to another person by driving a mechanically propelled vehicle dangerously on a road or other public place is guilty of an offence".[24] Similar provisions are contained in the French (Article 222-19-1)[25] and Polish (Article 177 of the Penal Code).[26]

In all the above-mentioned cases, the legislator ordered a penalty to be imposed for causing a road accident resulting in bodily injury. The addressee of such order is, first of all, a state authority (court). This does not mean, however, that they do not

[21] Ziembiński (1960), Ziembiński and Zieliński (1992).

[22] Alchourron and Bulygin (1971), Atienza and Manero (1998, p. 7), Rostalski (2019).

[23] German Criminal Code in the version published on 13 November 1998 (Federal Law Gazette I, p. 3322), as last amended by Article 2 of the Act of 22 November 2021, Federal Law Gazette I, p. 4906 (StGB), https://www.gesetze-im-internet.de/englisch_stgb/. Accessed 20 September 2023.

[24] Road Traffic Act 1988, UK Public General Acts 1988 c. 52, https://www.legislation.gov.uk/ukpga/1988/52/contents.

[25] Tomlinson (1999, p. 108).

[26] Act of 6 June 1997 The Polish Penal Code, Dz. U. 1997 Nr 88 poz. 553, with further amendments, https://www.imolin.org/doc/amlid/Poland_Penal_Code1.pdf.

contain any instructions addressed to the individual. It is possible to derive from the penalising provisions a general prohibition of engaging in risky behaviour that may lead to an accident. To recognise that a conduct is punishable implies that it is also prohibited. It is impossible to argue that a certain class of behaviour is punishable and allowed at the same time.[27]

The prohibition of excessively risky behaviour is not, however, a complete norm. It does not show how the addressee can behave in order to avoid liability for the effect. For this reason, it must be specified by provisions of a regulatory nature, rules of the art or indications of knowledge (for example, everyone knows that feeding a baby rice with vodka could be lethal for him). They indicate what behaviour is allowed. In the above-mentioned case, these will be the applicable road traffic rules. If the perpetrator follows them, and yet the result occurs,[28] it will not be possible to assign criminal liability. As long as the individual acts within the limits of such regulations, his behaviour cannot be subject to criminal liability, regardless of its consequences. The prohibition, derived from the provision of criminal law, is narrowed down here, limited by the content of non-penal regulations.[29]

Therefore, we can distinguish two elements of the norm of the individual: (1) general prohibition/order, derived from penalising provisions and (2) regulations restricting the content of the prohibition. Together, both elements constitute one penal norm of an individual. From the perspective of the character of the competencies required to establish them, they are not uniform in nature. Only the establishment of a prohibition/order related to the threat of imposing a penalty constitutes a form of exercising *ius puniendi*. The remaining elements of the norm, narrowing the content of the prohibition/order, are not directly related to the *ius puniendi*, although they affect the final shape of the premises for criminal liability.

3.3 The Norm of a Court (State Official)

Both the hypothesis and the disposition of the norm binding a court (state official[30]) are of a more complex nature than it was in the case of the norm of an individual. Schematically, it can be presented in the following way: if the individual breaks the binding norm (A) and there are additional premises for criminal liability (B), and there are no negative premises of criminal liability (B'), the court should (is

---

[27] Atienza and Manero (1998, p. 122), Kratochwil (1989, p. 73), Paulson (1988, p. 66).

[28] In addition to the breach of a rule of conduct, the conditions of so-called objective imputability (Objektive Zurechnung) will also have to be met in order to be held liable for causing an effect. However, these remain outside the scope of the norm binding on the individual, as they refer to criteria that are recognisable ex post. See inter alia: Roxin and Greco (2020, p. 442), Kuhlen (2011, p. 331).

[29] Kardas (2011, p. 271).

[30] Atienza and Manero (1998, p. 124).

empowered) impose a penalty on the individual within the limits prescribed by law (C).[31]

The hypothesis of the norm of the court consists of two categories of elements.

The first category includes the necessity to state that an individual violates the binding penal norm (A). Failure to prove that the norm has been exceeded makes it impossible to consider a given behaviour unlawful within the meaning of criminal law.[32] It follows from the above that the norm of individual has two functions. On the one hand, it defines the course of action of the individual. On the other hand, it is included in the content of a penal norm that binds the authority as a criterion of criminal law assessment. However, its content remains unchanged at both stages. The court must determine its content taking into account the circumstances that occurred at the time of the perpetrator's action, and not at the time of taking courts' conventional action (i.e. assigning criminal liability in the judgment).[33]

The second category includes strictly penal conditions. Here we should include, for example, the requirement to establish guilt at the time of committing the act, regulations ordering the exclusion of criminal liability of the insane or acting in self-defense.[34]

The above-described elements of the court's norms together constitute the premises for assigning criminal liability. Their joint submission will trigger the disposition of the norm which will be binding on the criminal court. Its content boils down to an order to impose a penalty, within the limits provided for by law.

Regulations consisting solely of the norm of the court (not derived from the norm of an individual) are, as a rule, penal in the strict sense. Establishing their content as part of the law-making process is usually one aspect of the exercise of *ius puniendi*. Thus, the penal norm binding the organ remains beyond the direct influence of the law-making activity of entities that do not dispose of the imperium. The exceptions are regulations concerning human rights, which will have a limiting effect on the content of the court's norm (see Sect. 5.2).

References

Aichele A, Renzikowski J, Rostalski F (2022) Normentheorie. Grundlage einer universalen Strafrechtsdogmatik. Buttenheimer Gespräche, 1st edn. Duncker & Humblot, Berlin

Alchourron CE, Bulygin E (1971) Normative systems. Springer, Vienna

Atienza M, Manero JR (1998) A theory of legal sentences. Springer, Dordrecht, Boston

Dąbrowska-Kardas M (2012) Analiza dyrektywalna przepisów części ogólnej kodeksu karnego [A directive analysis of the provisions of the general part of the Penal Code]. Warszawa

Duff RA, Green S (2011) Philosophical foundations of criminal law, 1st edn. Oxford University Press, Oxford, New York

[31] Paulson (1988, p. 69).

[32] Kardas (2012).

[33] Kratochwil (1989, pp. 25–28).

[34] Fletcher (2000, p. 411).

Fletcher GP (1998) Basic concepts of criminal law. Oxford University Press, New York
Fletcher GP (2000) Rethinking criminal law. Oxford University Press, Oxford, New York
Hallevy G (2010) A modern treatise on the principle of legality in criminal law. Springer Nat EBook. https://doi.org/10.1007/978-3-642-13714-3
Hart HLA, Green L, Raz J, Bulloch PA (2012) The concept of law, 3rd edn. Oxford University Press, Oxford, United Kingdom
Kardas P (2011) Zbieg przepisów ustawy o prawie karnym. Analiza teoretyczna [Conflict of laws in criminal law. A theoretical analysis]. Warszawa
Kardas P (2012) O relacjach między strukturą przestępstwa a dekodowanymi z przepisów prawa karnego strukturami normatywnymi [On the relationship between the structure of the crime and the normative structures decoded from criminal law provisions]. Czas Prawa Karnego Nauk Penal 16
Kelsen H (1957) What is justice?: justice, law, and politics in the mirror of science. University of California Press, New York
Kelsen H (1971) The pure theory of law and analytical jurisprudence. In: What is justice?: justice, law, and politics in the mirror of science. University of California Press, New York
Kratochwil FV (1989) Rules, norms, and decisions: on the conditions of practical and legal reasoning in international relations and domestic affairs. Cambridge University Press, Cambridge
Kuhlen L (2011) Objektive Zurechnung bei Rechtfertigungsgründen [Objective attribution in the case of justification]. In: Objektive Zurechnung bei Rechtfertigungsgründen [Objective attribution for justification reasons]. De Gruyter, pp 331–348
Paulson SL (1988) An empowerment theory of legal norms*. Ratio Juris 1:58–72. https://doi.org/10.1111/j.1467-9337.1988.tb00004.x
Pohl Ł (2007) Struktura normy sankcjonowanej w prawie karnym: zagadnienia ogólne [Structure of the criminal law sanctioned norm: general issues]. Wydawnictwo Naukowe Uniwersytetu im. Adama Mickiewicza
Raz J (1980) The concept of a legal system: an introduction to the theory of the legal system, Subsequent. Oxford University Press, USA, Oxford, New York
Rostalski F (2019) Der Tatbegriff im Strafrecht, 1st edn. Mohr Siebeck, Tübingen
Roxin C, Greco L (2020) Strafrecht Allgemeiner Teil Bd. 1: Grundlagen. Der Aufbau der Verbrechenslehre, 5., vollständig neu bearbeitete Edition. C.H. Beck, München
Satzger H (2017) International and European criminal law, 2nd edn. C.H. Beck, München, Oxford, Baden-Baden
Tomlinson EA (tran) (1999) The French penal code of 1994 as amended as of January 1, 1999. Fred B Rothman & Co, Littleton, Colo
von Wright GH (1963) Norm and action: a logical enquiry, 1st edn. Routledge and Kegan Paul, London
Weaver RL, Burkoff JM, Hancock C (2021) Criminal law: a contemporary approach, 4th edn. West Academic Press, St. Paul, MN
Wróbel W (2003) Zmiana normatywna i zasady intertemporalne w prawie karnym [Normative change and intertemporal rules in criminal law]. Kraków
Ziembiński Z, Zieliński M (1992) Dyrektywy i sposób ich wypowiadania [Directives and how they are expressed]. Zakład Semiotyki Logicznej Uniwersytetu Warszawskiego
Ziembiński Z (1960) Przepis prawny a norma prawna [Legal provision versus legal norm]. Legal prescription and rule of law
Zoll A (1990) O normie prawnej z punktu widzenia prawa karnego [On the legal norm from the point of view of criminal law]. Krak Stud Prawnicze XXIII:69–95

Chapter 4
Non-state Actors as Law-Makers

Abstract The category of non-state actors is heterogeneous in nature. From the perspective of this study, however, what is crucial is not their nature as participants in international relations, but the source of their authority to formulate normative statements. This chapter analyses three key sources of this power: delegation, consent of the subject and transfer of knowledge into the field of law.

Keywords Non-state actors · Delegation of power · Consent · Transfer of knowledge to the law

The above-described categories of norms are the result of a joint interpretation of many regulations. Until recently, this term was understood to mean provisions of national law. Today, the law-making process is dispersed and transnational.[1] The above phenomenon is collectively referred to as "transnational law-making".[2] Although it takes place at the supranational level, the formulated regulations do not affect only the traditionally understood subjects of international law.[3] They also shape the scope of rights and obligations of the individual.[4] His/her freedoms may be guaranteed at this level (human rights), but may also be limited. International law is no longer a law of states.[5]

A question should be asked to what extent their source can be laws formulated by the actor, who are not states.[6] Such entities taking part in the law-making process[7]

---

[1] Palombella (2015, p. 57), d'Aspremont (2011a, p. 23, d).

[2] Brolmann and Radi (2016, p. 57), d'Aspremont (2010, p. 175, 2011b, p. 3).

[3] d'Aspremont (2010, p. 176).

[4] Kleinlein (2011, p. 41).

[5] d'Aspremont (2011a, p. 23).

[6] On non-state-state actors in general see inter alia: Brolmann and Radi (2016, pp. 3, 42), Noortmann and Ryngaert (2010a).

[7] Kleinlein (2011, p. 41), Breton-Le Goff (2011, p. 248), d'Aspremont (2011c, p. 425).

D. Zając, *Non-state Actors Law-making and Domestic Criminal Law*,
SpringerBriefs in Law, https://doi.org/10.1007/978-3-031-47870-3_4

are not a homogeneous group. It includes international organisations of various character,[8] statutory bodies,[9] international tribunals and even entities that do not have subjectivity within the meaning of international law.[10]

For the purposes of this study, non-state actor will be defined as any international entity that is not a state.[11] From an *ius puniendi* perspective, this is where the key dividing line runs. States have a presumption of authority in this respect, other players must derive their competence from special circumstances.

Traditionally, a distinction is made between governmental international organisations, non-governmental international organisations, statutory bodies and other informal groups.[12] In practice, a growing group of actors is emerging that escapes such a classification. The European Union is seen as a non-state actor *sui generis*.[13] Moreover, such a division seems inadequate from the perspective of the issue of this study. To determine the impact of the law-making activity on the content of domestic penal norms, the genesis of non-state actor is not important. What is crucial, however, is the basis of its power to undertake law-making activity. This is because the nature of that basis will determine the extent to which the regulations themselves are effective. What is the source of the binding force of a statement is crucial to its usefulness in the process of interpreting penal norms. Three possibilities should be pointed out here.

Firstly, the competence to make normative statements may originate from a delegation of power, made by the state (see Sect. 4.1). Secondly, it may result from the consent of the addressee himself, as the addressee of the norm, to be bound by certain regulations (see Sect. 4.2). Thirdly, binding force is to be found in the nature of the regulations, which reflect indications of knowledge (see Sect. 4.3). For the power of the state over individuals is not unlimited. It is restricted not only by indications of human rights, but also by the right to self-determination belonging to the individual or by information about the surrounding world.

Each of the above sources of competence has different limitations. The correct identification of the basis of the subject's legislative power will make it possible to verify whether the statement in question has binding force (whether it will be able to become part of the norm).

---

[8] Noortmann and Ryngaert (2010b, p. 1), d'Aspremont (2010, p. 171, 2011b, p. 23), Collins (2011, p. 311).

[9] Ulfstein (2015, p. 250), Noortmann and Ryngaert (2010b).

[10] Brolmann and Radi (2016, p. 42), Muchlinski (2010, p. 9), Hernandez (2011, p. 140).

[11] Such a broad definition is not common in the literature. Rather, representatives of the doctrine apply a narrow understanding of the term "non-state actors". See, inter alia: d'Aspremont (2011a, p. 23), Kleinlein (2011, p. 41), Collins (2011, p. 311).

[12] Ulfstein (2015, p. 250).

[13] Wunderlich (2012, p. 653), Geiger (2015, p. 12).

4.1 Delegation of Power as a Basis for Law-Making Competence

Non-state actors may be empowered to make regulations with normative capacity—by virtue of delegation.[14] In this case, states transfer a certain amount of their sovereign powers, while declaring that they will submit to decisions, formulated by an empowered entity. The decisions of these entities shall be effective (have required capacity) under the principle *pacta sunt servanda.* A distinction should be made from delegation when the state makes use of regulations made by a non-state actor in the process of interpreting norms, but this actor has not been previously empowered to make such regulations. Examples of this type of regulation include the ISO standards (see Sect. 4.3).

The scope of the delegation determines which specific regulations a non-state actor can formulate.[15] From the perspective of the topic of the study, the delegation of competence to make regulations that may constitute elements of penal norms is of particular importance. Even so narrowly understood, the institution of delegation is still not characterised by homogeneity. In this respect, two axes of division can be distinguished.

Firstly, the delegation may entitle to the formulation of statements of a regulatory nature, without entering directly into the area of *ius puniendi*, or delegate the competence to define the criteria of criminal responsibility. The enactment of provisions imposing a specific obligation on an individual to act under threat of punishment will require the delegation of a broad competence, referring directly to the *ius puniendi.*[16] The fact that a non-state actor has acquired the power to regulate in a particular area does not mean that it can also criminalise breaking given regulation. Such competence cannot be presumed. In theory, it is possible to break with the concept of *ius puniendi* as *domaine réservé* and to transfer the complete competence to establish penal norms to a non-state actor. In practice, at the current stage of development, such a solution does not occur and is in fact undesirable, due to cultural differences. Even in the case

[14] Österdahl (2015, p. 124). On delegation see *inter alia*: Franchino (2007), Iancu (2014), Mégret (2020).

[15] For example, in accordance with the Article 290 of Consolidated version of the Treaty on the Functioning of the European Union, 13 December 2007, 2008/C 115/01 [TFEU], https://eur-lex.europa.eu/legal-content/EN/TXT/?uri=CELEX%3AC2008%2F115%2F01.: "1. A legislative act may delegate to the Commission the power to adopt non-legislative acts of general application to supplement or amend certain non-essential elements of the legislative act. The objectives, content, scope and duration of the delegation of power shall be explicitly defined in the legislative acts. The essential elements of an area shall be reserved for the legislative act and accordingly shall not be the subject of a delegation of power. 2. Legislative acts shall explicitly lay down the conditions to which the delegation is subject; these conditions may be as follows: (a) the European Parliament or the Council may decide to revoke the delegation; (b) the delegated act may enter into force only if no objection has been expressed by the European Parliament or the Council within a period set by the legislative act. For the purposes of (a) and (b), the European Parliament shall act by a majority of its component members, and the Council by a qualified majority. 3. The adjective "delegated" shall be inserted in the title of delegated acts". See inter alia: Iancu (2014, p. 272), Franchino (2007, p. 20).

[16] Iancu (2014, p. 96).

of the European Union, which is a *sui generis* entity with the power to regulate within a specific system (transnational legislation[17]), the legitimacy to law-making in the area of criminal law is significantly reduced.[18] In accordance with the Article 83 of the TFEU, the EU is entitled to introduce "minimum standards" of penalisation,[19] without any direct effectiveness. Theoretically, the possibility for non-state actors to make criminalisation decisions exists in two cases. Such law-making can be taken by the EU, on the basis of Article 325 TFEU, in the face of fraud affecting its fiscal interests.[20] Such a power may also be derived from the provisions of Chapter VII of the UN Charter, under which the UN Security Council may, inter alia, "decide what measures not involving the use of armed force are to be employed to give effect to its decisions, and it may call upon the Members of the United Nations to apply such measures".[21] These measures may also have the character of penal regulations. Since it makes it possible to formulate a power of military intervention, it is all the more likely to form the basis for penalising the behaviour of individuals insofar as it constitutes a threat to peace. Much more common is the delegation of directly binding acts of a regulatory nature. EU regulations are an example of this.

Secondly, looking from the perspective of the addressee, the delegation may empower the non-state actor to make regulations that are addressed to the state, or regulations that are directly effective on the individual. This distinction criterion is of key importance from the perspective of penal norms. If the non-state actor has not been empowered to regulate the behaviour of individuals, its statements will not be able to directly impinge on the content of a norm binding on the individual.

To the extent that the delegation empowers non-state actors to formulate regulations that are addressed to the state, they primarily have a vertical rather than a horizontal impact. They oblige the state to shape its internal penal policy accordingly—and are not concerns directly with interstate relations. However, this impact is not of a homogeneous nature—in this respect, a further division must be made.

Non-state actor may be entitled to formulate a modification of a state-binding international obligation. In this case, the addressee of the regulation is the state as the entity obligated to its implementation into national law.[22] For example, under Article 3[23] of the Convention on Narcotic Drugs, States Parties have delegated to the Commission on Narcotic Drugs under the United Nations Economic and Social

---

[17] Brolmann and Radi (2016, p. 61); Judgment of the Court of 15 July 1964, Flaminio Costa v E.N.E.L., Reference for a preliminary ruling: Giudice conciliatore di Milano-Italy, Case 6-64, https://eur-lex.europa.eu/legal-content/EN/TXT/?uri=CELEX%3A61964CJ0006; Ambos (2018, p. 23), Klip (2021, p. 228), Satzger (2017, p. 48).

[18] Toscano (2015, p. 35).

[19] Ambos (2018, p. 17), Toscano (2015, p. 39), Klip (2021, p. 228), Peristeridou (2011, p. 15).

[20] Klip (2021, p. 233), Ambos (2018, p. 19). The Author sets out the reasoning behind this interpretation of Article 335 TFEU.

[21] Charter of the United Nations, 24 October 1945, 1 UNTS XVI, https://treaties.un.org/doc/publication/ctc/uncharter.pdf.

[22] Klip (2021, p. 294).

[23] Single Convention on Narcotic Drugs 1961, UNTS, vol. 520, https://www.unodc.org/pdf/convention_1961_en.pdf.

Council the authority to update the list of prohibited drugs. The content of the list, which is shaped by the Commissions, in cooperation with the WHO,[24] is part of an international obligation requiring a state, among other things, to criminalise the traffic in such substances.[25] The Commission's decision is clearly fundamental to the content of both categories of penal norms. At the same time, it is neither directly binding on courts nor on individuals. In order for it to be taken into account in the decoding process, it will need to be implemented, if only by making an open reference at the level of national law. The decision itself does not yet constitute a statement capable of being an element of a penal norm. It is not addressed to any of the addressees of the criminal norms: neither the court nor the individual.

On the other hand, non-state actor also may be empowered to formulate regulations that influence state functionaries (courts) directly, as an element of penal norm of court. The most obvious example here is the delegation of law-making powers to EU bodies.[26] However, the delegation to a non-state actor competences to interpret a directly effective international agreement also has similar consequences. In this case, the non-state actor does not acquire the power to legislate directly. It is, however, empowered to exercise judicial law-making. This is particularly evident in the area of human rights. For example, judgments of the ECtHR, although binding in a specific case, give normative content to the general provisions of the ECHR. In practice, the Convention is treated by the domestic court as binding law.[27] The Convention does not indicate how it is to be implemented. In practice, States Parties consider it to be directly binding. It should be considered as a method of implementation, which is a

---

[24] UN General Assembly, Entry into force of the constitution of the World Health Organization, 17 November 1947, A/RES/131, https://digitallibrary.un.org/record/209903.

[25] For example: Single Convention on Narcotic Drugs 1961, UNTS, vol. 520, https://www.unodc.org/pdf/convention_1961_en.pdf. In the Article 36 of the Convention we can read: "1. (a) Subject to its constitutional limitations, each Party shall adopt such measures as will ensure that cultivation, production, manufacture, extraction, preparation, possession, offering, offering for sale, distribution, purchase, sale, delivery on any terms whatsoever, brokerage, dispatch, dispatch in transit, transport, importation and exportation of drugs contrary to the provisions of this Convention, and any other action which in the opinion of such Party may be contrary to the provisions of this Convention, shall be punishable offences when committed intentionally, and that serious offences shall be liable to adequate punishment particularly by imprisonment or other penalties of deprivation of liberty".

[26] For example under the Article 325 of TFEU. The Article has been changed in Lisbon Treaty. As Geiger and Khan indicate: "The most important change, however, was brought about by deleting the second sentence in paragraph 4, which stipulated: 'These measures shall not concern the application of national criminal law or the national administration of justice'. Together with the new Article 86 TFEU which creates the legal basis for establishing a European Public Prosecutor's Office for the protection of the Union's financial interests, this may be properly understood as an almost revolutionary act, since criminal law and procedure are widely considered cornerstones of state sovereignty"—Geiger and Khan (2015, p. 1009).

[27] Beijer (2017, p. 31); Ireland v United Kingdom, Admissibility, Merits, App No 5310/71, A/25, [1978] ECHR 1, (1979–80) 2 EHRR 25, IHRL 16 (ECHR 1978), 18 January 1978, ECHR, https://opil.ouplaw.com/display/10.1093/law:ihrl/16echr78.case.1/law-ihrl-16echr78. The Convention does not indicate how it is to be implemented. In practice, States Parties consider it to be directly binding. This practice should be considered as a method of implementation, which is a manifestation of the exercise of the international obligation described in Article 1 of the Convention.

manifestation of the exercise of the international obligation described in Article 1 of the Convention. At the same time, the ECtHR judgments are treated in practice as a source of its binding interpretation of Convention.[28] As Kleinlein indicates: "Functionally, human rights courts can be compared to domestic constitutional courts".[29] Their failure to be taken into account by the domestic court carries a high risk of an action by the individual, on the grounds of violation of the ECHR.[30] The regulations thus formulated affect the content of the penal norm of court (see points 4.3 and 5.1).

Delegation entitling to provide regulations binding on individuals is rare—viewed from the perspective of international law as a whole. Of course, for the EU Member States, such laws are a natural part of the legal system, however, the EU is the exception here, a globally unique entity. An example of such a regulation is the MAR Regulation,[31] which contains provisions specifying how business confidential information is to be handled. Its consideration became necessary in the process of determining the content of the penal norms (if an individual was bound by the regulation as a part of norm, an action in compliance with it could not constitute an offence[32]).

4.1.1 Exceeding the Delegation

What are the consequences of exceeding the delegation by non-state actor? Can a domestic court (or individual) refrain from taking given regulation into account if he considers that the scope of the delegation has been exceeded? The answer depends on a number of factors. The matter is further complicated by the fact that in many cases its scope of delegation will not be clear and the question of the binding (legal) nature of a particular statement will be the subject of dispute.[33]

In the case of an individual, this problem is marginal—the limited possibilities of making regulations directly binding on citizens mean that the problem will hardly arise in their case. In theory, there may be acts of EU law issued outside the scope of delegation. In practice, the shape of the legislative process within the Union itself partially eliminates such risks. In view of the existence of formal control mechanisms, it must be assumed that the individual does not have the power to assess for himself whether an act has been issued by a non-state is outside the scope of the delegation.

[28] Harmsen (2007, p. 36).

[29] Kleinlein (2011, p. 41). See also: Harmsen (2007, p. 33).

[30] Beijer (2017, p. 32).

[31] Regulation (EU) No 596/2014 of the European Parliament and of the Council of 16 April 2014 on market abuse (market abuse regulation) and repealing Directive 2003/6/EC of the European Parliament and of the Council and Commission Directives 2003/124/EC, 2003/125/EC and 2004/72/EC Text with EEA relevance, https://eur-lex.europa.eu/legal-content/EN/TXT/?uri=celex%3A32014R0596.

[32] Satzger (2017, p. 98).

[33] Ulfstein (2015, p. 252).

By analogy, as is the case with national law (e.g. implementing acts), such verification must be carried out by the authority.

The issue becomes more complicated when viewed from the perspective of the court (state authorities). The following considerations should be pointed out here. Firstly, the action taken by non-state actors is usually subject to scrutiny by states under the relevant procedure. They are given either the possibility to raise objections (e.g. the mechanism formulated in Article 3 (8) of the Convention on Narcotic Drugs[34]) or the right to appeal to a body verifying the correctness of a specific law-making activity (e.g. the Court of Justice of the European Union[35]). Where formal methods exist to control action within the limits of delegation, these should be used first. Secondly, allowing the use of diffuse control carries risks in the area of international relations. National courts, which are responsible for exercising the *ius puniendi*, do not, as a rule, have the competence to carry out this type of verification. Theoretically, the right to carry out such a verification may derive from internal regulations. However, adopting this solution entails the risk of discrepancies in the application of the law and the creation of further tensions at international level.

Its sure that delegation of power is not the only source of authority for regulation by non-state actors.[36] They often do not have powers inherent in the sphere of the imperium[37] and yet formulate regulations, acting outside democratic legitimacy.[38] It leads us to the next two issues: limiting and exceeding the delegation.

4.1.2 Limits of Delegation

In the above context, the question of the limits of delegation arises. This issue has been discussed extensively on the occasion of the work on the creation of the International Criminal Court.[39] A provocative question may be asked: is it possible for a State to

[34] Single Convention on Narcotic Drugs 1961, UNTS, vol. 520, https://www.unodc.org/pdf/convention_1961_en.pdf. In accordance with the Article 3 (8a): "8. (a) The decisions of the Commission amending any of the Schedules shall be subject to review by the Council upon the request of any Party filed within ninety days from receipt of notification of the decision. The request for review shall be sent to the Secretary-General together with all relevant information upon which the request for review is based".

[35] Consolidated version of the Treaty on the Functioning of the European Union, 13 December 2007, 2008/C 115/01 [TFEU], https://eur-lex.europa.eu/legal-content/EN/TXT/?uri=CELEX%3AC2008%2F115%2F01. In accordance with Article 263 of the TFEU: "The Court of Justice of the European Union shall review the legality of legislative acts, of acts of the Council, of the Commission and of the European Central Bank, other than recommendations and opinions, and of acts of the European Parliament and of the European Council intended to produce legal effects vis-à-vis third parties. It shall also review the legality of acts of bodies, offices or agencies of the Union intended to produce legal effects vis-à-vis third parties".

[36] Brolmann and Radi (2016, p. 6), Palombella (2015), Österdahl (2015, p. 126).

[37] Österdahl (2015, p. 124).

[38] Pauwelyn et al. (2015, p. 97).

[39] Alter (2006, p. 312).

delegate the competence to exercise the right to punish (at the level of law-making or law-enforcement) to an international non-governmental organisation?

Firstly, in the situation outlined, there would be a deprivation of state influence over the decisions of a legitimate entity. INGOs do not (do not have to) act on the basis of national/domestic law of the delegating state. The only limitation here, depending on the will of the state, would in fact be the limits of delegation. This means that a particular aspect of the law of punishment would be exercised before an entity independent of the state, while the state would—by way of self-restraint—commit itself to accepting its decisions. From an international law perspective, this would amount to a relinquishment of an important range of sovereignty powers.

Secondly, such a decision would directly affect the situations of individuals, subordinate to the state. A private international actor would acquire the power to make rules, the violation of which was linked to the possibility of punishment. Citizens of the delegating state would be subject to the decisions of the non-state actor—by the very fact of their statehood. In this perspective, the relationship between the public and the private would be disrupted. Taking the democratic system as a point of reference, a peculiar loop becomes apparent: society places power in the hands of its representatives, who in turn delegate it to another external entity, which is already outside any democratic control. This is because such control is precluded by the private nature of the subject. For the above reasons, the solution outlined above would be in flagrant contradiction with the fundamental assumptions of democratic systems as expressed at the constitutional level.

It is against this background that the framework of requirements to be met by the delegation in the exercise of the right of punishment is outlined.

Firstly, the entity taking over the competence must not be non-state (private, non-governmental). The public nature of the entity, at least in principle, provides guarantees that in its actions it will pursue public objectives, taking into account the broad interests of society, and not exclusively corporate objectives.

Secondly, the exercise of the right to punish by a non-state actor will raise fewer doubts, the stronger the legitimacy to exercise power lies on the side of the entitled entity.

4.2 Consent of the Subject as a Basis for Law-Making Competence

The source of force of statements made by non-state actors may be the will of the actors who agree to be bound by certain regulations. Such consent may take the institutional form of a political decision, shaping internal law, or it may be a statement of individual will.

In the first case, such will is expressed on the basis of primary legitimacy, deriving from sovereignty.[40] This mechanism is not controversial; it is the essence of the

[40] Kratochwil (2015, p. 53).

exercise of state authority. Importantly, in order to give consent of this type, it is necessary to have legislative competence, which the court, as the addressee of the penal norm, is deprived of. If the legislature fails to implement them properly, the court will only be able to take these regulations into account if their content is within the limits of the applicable law.[41] They may serve as an argument in interpretation "hard-binding" law. Two issues are relevant here. First, it is not an infringement of the law for a national court to refuse to take them into account when interpreting a penal norm. Secondly, in interpreting the law, a criminal court is bound by the prohibition on the use of expansive interpretation to the detriment of the offender. As will be shown in the course of further considerations, the same non-state actor regulation will narrow the scope of criminalisation in one situation and lead to its expansion in another (see Sect. 4.2). This means that, depending on the context, its inclusion in the penal norm will be possible or excluded.

An example of law-making activity of the first category is the work of The Human Rights Committee (HCR), which is the statutory body of the ICCPR.[42] It is an example of an entity established by the will of states, to which no explicit law-making powers have been delegated.[43] Its statements do not indicate specific solutions, but only set out general assumptions, leaving states parties free to shape their own legal system.[44] Among other things, the HCR has the power to formulate General Comments[45], which are proposals for interpreting the provisions of the ICCPR. The mechanism of the impact of the HRC's provisions is described in the ICJ's reasoning in Diallo case: "Although the Court is in no way obliged, in the exercise of its judicial functions, to model its own interpretation of the Covenant on that of the Committee, it believes that it should ascribe great weight to the interpretation adopted by this independent body that was established specifically to supervise the application of that treaty. The point here is to achieve the necessary clarity and the essential consistency of international law, as well as legal security, to which both the individuals with guaranteed rights and the States obliged to comply with treaty obligations are entitled".[46] The HCR does not exercise imperium. The attribution

---

[41] Brolmann and Radi (2016, p. 37).

[42] UN General Assembly, International Covenant on Civil and Political Rights, 16 December 1966, United Nations, Treaty Series, vol. 999, p. 171 [ICCPR], https://treaties.un.org/doc/Treaties/1976/03/19760323%2006-17%20AM/Ch_IV_04.pdf. Article 28.1. of the ICCPR indicates: "There shall be established a Human Rights Committee (hereafter referred to in the present Covenant as the Committee). It shall consist of eighteen members and shall carry out the functions hereinafter provided".

[43] Ulfstein (2015, p. 252).

[44] Ibid., p. 251.

[45] In accordance with the Article 40 (4) of the ICCPR: "The Committee shall study the reports submitted by the States Parties to the present Covenant. It shall transmit its reports, and such general comments as it may consider appropriate, to the States Parties".

[46] The above is not modified by the interpretation of the HRC, in which the Committee pushes the thesis of the binding nature of its statements, see: UN Human Rights Committee, General comment no. 33, Obligations of States parties under the Optional Protocol to the International Covenant on Civil and Political Rights, 25 June 2009, CCPR/C/GC/33, https://documents-dds-ny.un.org/doc/UNDOC/GEN/G09/432/66/PDF/G0943266.pdf?OpenElement, p. 3. The document indicates: "The

of the HCR's statements as effective law depends solely on the political decision of a particular state. By the sovereign decision it may shape domestic legal system accordingly to the HCR's indications.

Where regulations of non-state actors, formulated outside the scope of delegation, directly affect the way in which individuals behave, the source of their binding force may be the consent of the individual. This may be expressed formally, e.g. by a declaration to abide by certain rules of procedure or, implicitly,[47] by the mere fact of undertaking a certain activity. In this case, we are not dealing with second-order standards issued by delegation, but with primary regulations.[48] The legislative activity of FIFA[49] or the IOC[50] can serve as an example of the first situation. Both entities are non-governmental international organisations responsible for the organisation of sports competitions. Their remit, as organiser of the event, includes, among other things, defining anti-doping regulations.[51] Regulations provided in this regard by both entities do not have the value of the law, issued under imperium. They are more like rules of the game, the violation of which may entail elimination from the competition. They are traditionally regarded as soft law regulations.[52] However, their role is not limited to playing time. They may constitute elements of a penal norm, being the basis for the assessment of an individual's behaviour in the framework of criminal proceedings (e.g. in a doping or cheating case). Consent will also be a source of "binding" force of normative statements wherever certain aspects of social life are regulated by private entities, in the face of the passivity of states or the impossibility of reaching consensus at the international level. Examples of this type of solution are regulations issued by bodies such as ICANN[53] or the standards of conduct that make

character of the views of the Committee is further determined by the obligation of States parties to act in good faith, both in their participation in the procedures under the Optional Protocol and in relation to the Covenant itself".

[47] Pauwelyn et al. (2015, pp. 86, 98), Klabbers et al. (2011, p. 114).

[48] Pauwelyn et al. (2015, p. 90).

[49] Urueña (2015, p. 150).

[50] See inter alia: Bowersox (2022, p. 456).

[51] International Olympic Committee, Anti-Doping Rules, applicable to the XXIV Olympic Winter Games, Beijing 2022, (as of November 2021), https://www.wada-ama.org/sites/default/files/resources/files/ioc_anti-doping_rules_applicable_to_the_xxiv_olympic_winter_games_clean_november_2021.pdf.

[52] Brolmann and Radi (2016, p. 29).

[53] Österdahl (2015, p. 125). The example of ICANN is symptomatic here—cyberspace, which escapes state jurisdiction, has been subject to specific standards that to some extent bind the entities operating in it.

up CSR[54] do not find a foothold in the will of states.[55] They have been developed on the basis of the practices of private entities.[56]

The consent of the individual is not a strong basis for the normative capacity of the provision, it is not absolute. In particular, it does not allow for the regulation of matters that remain in the sphere of the imperium. However, as long as non-state actor regulations remain within the limits of the individual right of self-determination (individual freedoms, freedoms to self-endangerment, etc.), the court in the process of establishing penal norms will be bound by their content. If such a limit is exceeded, the court should refuse to apply the regulation in question in the process of interpreting penal norms. Illustrating the above with an example: suppose that the International Russian Roulette Association was formed and during the course of the game one of the participants suffered a death. In the process of decoding the norm, the court could disregard the rules of the game if it came to the conclusion that such a degree of self-endangerment is impermissible.[57]

4.3 Non-state Actor Law-Making as a Transfer of Knowledge into the Area of Norms

The binding force of non-state actor regulations may also be based on their relationship to the state of the art in given field. Very often such regulations are in fact the fruit of knowledge transfer to the law level and are technocratic in nature.[58] The aim of the law-making bodies is not to create a regulation that is binding (characterised by normative capacity) with the force of an imperium, but merely a guide indicating the optimal way to act.[59] From the perspective of criminal liability, however, such

---

[54] Noortmann and Ryngaert (2010b, p. 2), Davarnejad (2010)—as Autor indicates: "As the international legal personality of MNEs [Multinational Enterprise Groups-DZ] is generally not recognized, they are not obliged to respect human rights, labour or environmental standards imposed by international law. Therefore, some international law experts speak of a legal vacuum (or an accountability gap with reference to MNEs. The CRS notion encompasses the call for a corporate responsibility to respect human rights, social and environmental standards". In this perspective CRS plays similar role to human rights—limiting power of corporation.

[55] Brolmann and Radi (2016, p. 59); Gordon K, *The OECD Guidelines and Other Corporate Responsibility Instruments: A Comparison,* https://www.oecd.org/corporate/mne/WP-2001_5.pdf, 1 December 2001. However, it should be stressed that these principles have been partly codified in the OECD's activities—and to that extent have been shaped by the will of states—see *inter alia*: Davarnejad (2010, p. 55).

[56] Brolmann and Radi (2016, p. 29).

[57] On this topic broad: Feinberg (1989).

[58] Ibid., p. 90.

[59] GHTF Study Group 1 (2005) Essential Principles of Safety and Performance of Medical Devices GHTF Study Group 1 Endorsed by The Global Harmonization Task Force, https://www.imdrf.org/sites/default/files/docs/ghtf/final/sg1/technical-docs/ghtf-sg1-n41r9-2008-principles-safety-performance-050520.pdf. The introduction indicates that the guidance contained in the document is non-binding.

regulations introduce a kind of presumption of compliance with the rules of art. If the perpetrator has acted in accordance with the standard described by the expert body, the law binding on him at the time of the act must be deemed not to have been violated. Examples of such regulations are the standards formulated by the International Organisation for Standardisation (ISO).[60] In this perspective, the regulations issued by non-state actors are somewhat reminiscent of expert witness opinions, which are formulated *ex ante* and in a general and abstract manner.[61]

Law-making of this type essentially fills a normative vacuum. Regulations are used in the process of decoding the penal norm, because they often represent the best possible description of how the situation should have been handled. This has important consequences for interpretation of penal norms.

Firstly, the regulation issued on this base must give way to the legal standards established under the imperium of the state. If an issue is regulated differently by those with democratic legitimacy, it is this regulation that will have to be taken into account when determining the content of the penal norms. Secondly, they cannot directly affect the shape of the *ius puniendi*—as they are not given by virtue of the imperium. Thirdly, international standards are usually developed by expert bodies in highly developed countries. Meeting them will often be impossible in developing countries with different levels of wealth. In this situation, the international standard should be adapted to local conditions at the stage of application of the law, e.g. taking into account the indications of an expert opinion, which should indicate what standard is accepted in practice. The law must not establish requirements that are impossible to meet. In such cases, the court should refuse to apply them in the process of interpreting the standard.

Such law-making activity also carries risks due to the deficit of democratic control. When formulating recommendations/opinions/standards,[62] the non-state actor not only has expert knowledge,[63] but also represents certain interests. At the same time, the high degree of specialisation in the particular areas of life affected by regulation means that the boundary between the criteria of knowledge and interest is blurred.[64] And this circumstance should not be without influence on the court's assessment of the normative value of the discussed regulation.

---

[60] Palombella (2015, p. 61). See also: Statutes of International Organization for Standardization, 2022, https://www.iso.org/files/live/sites/isoorg/files/archive/pdf/en/statutes.pdf; The British Standards Institution, A standard for standards. Principles of standardization, BS 0:2011, https://www.bsigroup.com/LocalFiles/en-GB/standards/bs0-pas0/BSI-BS0-Standard-for-Standards-UK-EN.pdf.

[61] Pauwelyn et al. (2015, p. 94).

[62] Palombella (2015, p. 65).

[63] Pauwelyn et al. (2015).

[64] Kratochwil (2015, p. 55).

References

Acquaviva G (2011) Non-state actors from the perspective of international criminal tribunals. In: d'Aspremont J (ed) Participants in the international legal system: multiple perspectives on non-state actors in international law. Routledge, London

Alter KJ (2006) Delegation to international courts and the limits of re-contracting political power. In: Nielson DL, Hawkins DG, Lake DA, Tierney MJ (eds) Delegation and agency in international organizations. Cambridge University Press, Cambridge, pp 312–338

Ambos K (2018) European criminal law. Cambridge University Press, Cambridge

Beijer M (2017) Limits of fundamental rights protection by the EU: the scope for the development of positive obligations. Intersentia, Cambridge, Antwerp, Portland

Bowersox Z (2022) Workers' rights and the Olympic games: the international Olympic committee and institutional law making. Calif West Int Law J 52

Breton-Le Goff G (2011) NGOs' perspectives on non-state actors. In: d'Aspremont J (ed) Participants in the international legal system: multiple perspectives on non-state actors in international law. Routledge, London

Brolmann C, Radi Y (2016) Research handbook on the theory and practice of international lawmaking. Edward Elgar Publishing, Cheltenham, UK Northhampton, MA, USA

Collins R (2011) Non-state actors in international institutional law: non-state, inter-state or supra-state? The peculiar identity of the intergovernmental organization. In: d'Aspremont J (ed) Participants in the international legal system: multiple perspectives on non-state actors in international law. Routledge, London

d'Aspremont J (2010) International law-making by non-state actors: changing the model or putting the phenomenon into perspective? In: Noortmann M, Ryngaert C (eds) Non-state actor dynamics in international law: from law-takers to law-makers. Routledge, Farnham

d'Aspremont J (2011a) Non-state actors from the perspective of legal positivism. The communitarian semantics for the secondary rules of international law. In: d'Aspremont J (ed) Participants in the international legal system: multiple perspectives on non-state actors in international law. Routledge, London

d'Aspremont J (2011b) Non-state actors in international law: oscillating between concepts and dynamics. In: d'Aspremont J (ed) Participants in the international legal system: multiple perspectives on non-state actors in international law. Routledge, London

d'Aspremont J (2011c) Conclusion: inclusive law-making and law-enforcement processes for an exclusive international legal system. In: d'Aspremont J (ed) Participants in the international legal system: multiple perspectives on non-state actors in international law. Routledge, London

d'Aspremont J (2011d) The politics of deformalization in international law. Goettingen J Int Law. https://doi.org/10.3249/1868-1581-3-2-ASPREMONT

Davarnejad L (2010) The impact of non-state actors on the international law regime of corporate social responsibility: blessing or curse? In: Noortmann M, Ryngaert C (eds) Non-state actor dynamics in international law: from law-takers to law-makers. Routledge, Farnham

Feinberg J (1989) Harm to self, Reprint. Oxford University Press, New York

Franchino F (2007) The powers of the union: delegation in the EU. Cambridge University Press, Cambridge, New York

Geiger R (2015) Framework, goals and bases of the EU. In: Geiger R, Khan D-E, Kotzur M (eds) European Union treaties: a commentary: treaty on European Union—treaty on the functioning of the European Union—charter of fundamental rights of the European Union. München, Oxford

Geiger R, Khan D-E (2015) Combating fraud. In: Geiger R, Khan D-E, Kotzur M (eds) European Union treaties: a commentary: treaty on European Union—treaty on the functioning of the European Union—charter of fundamental rights of the European Union. München, Germany, Oxford

Harmsen R (2007) The European court of human rights as a "constitutional court". In: Morison J, McEvoy K, Anthony G (eds) Judges, transition, and human rights, 1st edn. Oxford University Press, Oxford, New York

Hernandez G (2011) Non-state actors from the perspective of the international court of justice. In: d'Aspremont J (ed) Participants in the international legal system: multiple perspectives on non-state actors in international law. Routledge, London

Iancu B (2014) Legislative delegation: the erosion of normative limits in modern constitutionalism. Springer, Berlin Heidelberg

Klabbers J, Peters A, Ulfstein G (2011) The constitutionalization of international law. Oxford University Press, Oxford, New York

Kleinlein T (2011) Non-state actors from an international constitutionalist perspective. Participation matters! In: d'Aspremont J (ed) Participants in the international legal system: multiple perspectives on non-state actors in international law. Routledge, London

Klip A (2021) European criminal law: an integrative approach, 4th edn. Intersentia, Cambridge Antwerp Chicago

Kratochwil F (2015) Legalism and the 'dark' side of global governance. In: Liivoja R, Petman J (eds) International law-making: essays in honour of Jan Klabbers, 1st edn. Routledge, Abingdon, Oxon

Mégret F (2020) The international criminal court: between international ius puniendi and state delegation. Max Planck Yearb U N Law Online 23:161–220. https://doi.org/10.1163/18757413_023001007

Muchlinski P (2010) Multinational enterprises as actors in international law: creating 'Soft Law' obligations and 'Hard Law' rights. In: Noortmann M, Ryngaert C (eds) Non-state actor dynamics in international law: from law-takers to law-makers. Routledge, Farnham

Noortmann M, Ryngaert C (2010a) Non-state actor dynamics in international law: From law-takers to lawmakers. Routledge, Farnham

Noortmann M, Ryngaert C (2010b) Introduction: non-state actors: international law's problematic case and Cedric Ryngaert. In: Noortmann M, Ryngaert C (eds) Non-state actor dynamics in international law: from law-takers to law-makers. Routledge, Farnham

Österdahl I (2015) (International) Law! In: Liivoja R, Petman J (eds) International law-making: essays in honour of Jan Klabbers, 1st edn. Routledge, Abingdon, Oxon

Palombella G (2015) Global legislation and its discontents. In: Liivoja R, Petman J (eds) International law-making: essays in honour of Jan Klabbers, 1st edn. Routledge, Abingdon, Oxon

Pauwelyn J, Wessel RA, Wouters J (2015) Informal international law as presumptive law. In: Liivoja R, Petman J (eds) International law-making: essays in honour of Jan Klabbers, 1st edn. Routledge, Abingdon, Oxon

Peristeridou C (2011) The principle of lex certa in national law and European perspectives. In: Klip A (ed) Substantive criminal law of the European Union. Maklu, Antwerpen

Satzger H (2017) International and European criminal law, 2nd edn. C.H. Beck, München, Oxford, Baden-Baden

Toscano G (2015) The principle of Nullum Crimen Sine Lege in the construction of European criminal law. In: Ruggeri S (ed) Human rights in European criminal law: new developments in European legislation and case law after the Lisbon treaty, 2015th edn. Springer, New York, NY

Ulfstein G (2015) Law-making by human rights treaty bodies. In: Liivoja R, Petman J (eds) International law-making: essays in honour of Jan Klabbers, 1st edn. Routledge, Abingdon, Oxon

Urueña R (2015) Law-making through comparative international law? In: Liivoja R, Petman J (eds) International law-making: essays in honour of Jan Klabbers, 1st edn. Routledge, Abingdon, Oxon

Wunderlich J-U (2012) The EU an Actor Sui Generis? A comparison of EU and ASEAN actorness*. JCMS J Common Mark Stud 50:653–669. https://doi.org/10.1111/j.1468-5965.2011.02237.x

Chapter 5
Regulation Issued by the Non-state Actors

Abstract Statements made by non-state actors are characterised by great diversity. They may have direct effect or require implementation through a national legislative decision. Their addressees (state, court, individual) vary. They may contain self-contained regulations or have only interpretative value. This chapter is devoted to their typology, taking into account the key criteria for the interpretation of penal norms.

Keywords Addressee of the penal norms · Non-binding international law · Soft law · Implementation · Human rights

Regulations enacted by non-state actors form a kind of collage of seemingly unrelated directives of a diverse nature. On the one hand, non-state actors formulate recommendations or opinions—which are in fact *de lege ferenda* postulates.[1] At the same time, they participate in the process of creating regulations constituting sources of law within the meaning of Art. 38 of the ICJ Statute[2]: treaties,[3] judicial decisions[4]

---

[1] Koskenniemi (2015, p. 18), Kratochwil (2015, pp. 44, 56), Brolmann and Radi (2016, p. 26), d'Aspremont (2011).

[2] d'Aspremont (2011, p. 511).

[3] Brolmann and Radi (2016, p. 50), Fitzmaurice (2015, p. 193); Vienna Convention on the Protection of Ozone Layer, 22 March 1985, in force 22 September 1988, 1513 UNTS 323, https://treaties.un.org/doc/Treaties/1988/09/19880922%2003-14%20AM/Ch_XXVII_02p.pdf. An example of this type of activity is that of the Conference of the Parties, which is treaty body of The Vienna Convention for the Protection of the Ozone Layer. The body has the power to formulate Protocols to the underlying agreements, which are then adopted by a majority of the pacting states. In the Article 9 (4) of the Convention, we can read: "The procedure mentioned in paragraph 3 above shall apply to amendments to any protocol, except that a two-thirds majority of the parties to that protocol present and voting at the meeting shall suffice for their adoption". This is how, for example, the content of the Montreal Protocol, mandating a ban on the import of certain environmentally harmful substances, was established. See: Montreal Protocol on Substances that Deplete the Ozone Layer, 16 September 1987, in force 1 January 1989, 1522 UNTS 3, https://treaties.un.org/doc/publication/unts/volume%201522/volume-1522-i-26369-english.pdf.

[4] Hernandez (2016, p. 200), Bogdandy and Venzke (2012, p. 3).

D. Zając, *Non-state Actors Law-making and Domestic Criminal Law*,
SpringerBriefs in Law, https://doi.org/10.1007/978-3-031-47870-3_5

and the teachings.[5] This makes it difficult to carry out a collective analysis of them in order to determine their impact on the content of penal norms. Dividing the complex set into smaller subgroups, using criteria relevant from the perspective of their impact on *ius puniendi*, will allow one to fully perceive the diversity of its elements. The analysis presented below views the regulations from a vertical perspective, as being part of a system whose core is—in principle—domestic law.[6] The typology is not logical, but substantive. The same element therefore belongs to many subsets at the same time. Only by considering all its features together will it be possible to determine unequivocally how its establishment will affect the way in which *ius puniendi* is exercised.

5.1 Regulations Requiring Action by the National Legislator and Regulations Directly Affecting the Addressee of a Penal Norm

Determining whether a particular statement by a non-state actor can constitute an element of a penal norm binding on the addressee (court or individual) is of crucial importance in the process of applying domestic criminal law. Depending on the nature of the regulation, it will already be binding for the individual/court at the moment of its formulation at the international level or only upon a decision by the legislature (dualistic model) or the constitutional power (monistic model).[7]

Examples of statements directly affecting the addressee of the penal norm are EU laws with direct effect,[8] but also, for example, ISO standards[9] or judgments of international courts, as well as some regulations in the area of human rights. The effectiveness of normative statements in this case does not depend on the activity of the legislative/constitutional power. The lack of relevant implementing legislation will not exclude the use of this category of regulations with respect to the addressees bound by them. Where the regulation has the character of a court judgment or will

---

[5] Creutz (2015, p. 171). An example of this type of action is, for example, the activity of The International Commission on Intervention and State Sovereignty (ICISS), which in 2001 clarified the definition of the responsibility to protect, adopted at the UN Summit in 2005 as part of the UN General Assembly resolution. World Summit Outcome Document (WSOD) in paragraph 139 indicated that: "The international community, through the United Nations, also has the responsibility to use appropriate diplomatic, humanitarian and other peaceful means, in accordance with Chapters VI and VIII of the Charter, to help to protect populations from genocide, war crimes, ethnic cleansing and crimes against humanity".—https://www.un.org/en/development/desa/population/migration/generalassembly/docs/globalcompact/A_RES_60_1.pdf.

[6] Österdahl (2015, p. 130).

[7] See for example: Crawford (2019, p. 45).

[8] Geiger (2015, p. 13); Judgment of The European Court of Justice, Van Gend & Loos, Case 26-62 (5 February 1963), https://eur-lex.europa.eu/legal-content/EN/TXT/?uri=celex%3A61962CJ0026.

[9] Fontanelli (2011). The Author explains migration of ISO standards onto the binding regulations of international trade law.

be the result of the process of informal law-making, there its use in the process of decoding penal norms will be similar in both monistic and dualistic systems. It is aptly pointed out by Osterdahl that: "Non-binding international law will not have to be ratified by the domestic legislative assemblies making it easier to implement than binding law, such as treaties".[10] In the above cases, the regulations of non-state actor may be incorporated directly into the penal norms, as their elements. In doing so, it should be borne in mind that not every regulation that is binding on the court can also be considered binding on the individual (see Sect. 5.2). This will have important consequences in the process of interpreting penal norms.

Much more often, the legal effectiveness of the statements of non-state actors requires their formal introduction into the national legal system through the national law-making process. The legislative authority gives them a form that binds the individual and/or the court. An example of a statement of this type is the addition to the list of prohibited substances by the UN Commission (see Sect. 4.1). It does not constitute a sui generis regulation, but clarifies the content of an international obligation subject to implementation.

Against this background, the difference between a monistic and a dualistic system is drawn.

Describing monism, Crawford indicates: "Monism postulates that national and international law form one single legal order, or at least a number of interlocking orders which should be presumed to be coherent and consistent. On that basis, international law can be applied directly within the national legal order".[11] As a consequence we can say that monism presupposes that the regulation of international law, insofar as it is binding, must be taken into account in the interpretation of national norms. Here, implementation is of a general, collective nature.

On the other side, in Crawford approach dualism is characterised as follows: "Dualism emphasizes the distinct and independent character of the international and national legal systems. International law is seen as a law between states whereas national law applies within a state, regulating the relations of its citizens with each other and with that state. Neither legal order has the power to create or alter rules of the other. When an international law rule applies, this is because a rule of the national legal system so provides. In the case of a conflict between international law and national law, the dualist would assume that a national court would apply national law, or at least that it is for the national system to decide which rule is to prevail".[12] It means that in the pure dualistic system the legislature intervenes in each case when international regulations are used within internal relations.

However, even in the case of monistic systems, direct application will often be impossible due to the content of the regulations. Their addressee is primarily the state, as a subject of international relations. Non-state actors do not refer them to its individual organs or individuals. In practice, this makes it impossible to unequivocally

---

[10] Österdahl (2015, p. 124).

[11] Crawford (2019, p. 45).

[12] Ibid., p. 45.

recognise whether the addressee of the given regulation is any of the addressees of the penal norms.

5.2 Regulations Affecting the Individual and Regulations Affecting the Court

Determining who is the addressee of a regulation is crucial in the process of interpreting penal norms. If a particular regulation binds only state authorities, it cannot be used in the process of decoding a norm that binds the individual. This, in turn, will limit its ability to influence the shape of the prerequisites for criminal liability (see Sects. 3.1 and 6.1).

In the traditional view, an individual is not bound by international law.[13] The citizen is under the authority of the state and it is through the decisions of its authorities that he or she may be affected by the content of the international provisions. In practice, however, there will be situations in which the individual is directly bound by non-state actors' regulations.

This will happen in five situations. First, where a non-state actor obtains the competence to make such rules by virtue of a delegation (see Sect. 4.1). Second, where an individual consents (however implicitly) to be bound by particular regulations (see Sect. 4.2). Third, where the specified regulation will constitute a transfer of knowledge to the standards level (see Sect. 4.3). Fourth, where the individual will be acting as a state official. For example, a judgment of an international tribunal, defining what is the illegal push-back in the sense of international law, impinges not only on the conduct of the state, but also on its functionaries, who should strictly refrain from the conduct referred to in the judgment (see Sect. 6.1 and further considerations in this section). Fifth, where the regulation will bind the authority of the state, expanding the sphere of individual freedom. For example, if a judgment of an international tribunal deems a particular national regulation/practice to violate the right to assembly, an individual will be able to participate in assemblies by invoking the content of international law, regardless of the national regulation.[14] In this case, the individual is not directly addressed by the regulation, but benefits from a limitation of the state's arbitrariness (see Sect. 6.1). Indeed, in Western culture there is a presumption of individual freedom. If something is not forbidden, it should be considered

---

[13] Ibid., p. 111. But the Author indicates: "There is no general rule that the individuals cannot be 'subjects of international law', and in particular contexts individuals may have rights which they can vindicate by international action, notably in the field of human rights and investment protection".

[14] A regulation of particular importance here is Article 11 of European Convention for the Protection of Human Rights and Fundamental Freedoms, as amended by Protocols Nos. 11 and 14, 4 November 1950, ETS 5, https://www.echr.coe.int/documents/d/echr/convention_ENG, developed by ECtHR case law. See inter alia: Guide on the case-law of the European Convention on Human Rights. Mass protests. Updated on 31 August 2022, https://www.echr.coe.int/documents/d/echr/Guide_Mass_protests_ENG; Guide on Article 11 of the European Convention on Human Rights Freedom of assembly and association, https://www.echr.coe.int/documents/d/echr/guide_art_11_eng.

permitted. Human rights, therefore, do not contain a permission, but a prohibition addressed to the state to impose certain prohibitions, limiting the freedom of the individual.[15]

Broader group is the regulations of non-state actors, which are addressed to the court (state authorities). The state, on the one hand, is the actor responsible for the execution of the *ius puniendi*; on the other hand, it is the most important subject of international law. Both of these facts make the state the main recipient of regulations that shape criminal law. Here, the regulations of international law shape the manner of conduct not so much horizontally, as a member of the international community, but vertically, projecting the manner of conduct with entities subject to its imperium. This conduct does not manifest itself in the activity of an abstractly understood actor, but of its concrete organs—police, prosecutors' offices, courts, etc. It therefore seems crucial to establish the premises for the binding of state authorities to regulations established by non-state actors.[16]

Firstly, the influence on the content of the norm binding the authority takes place indirectly. The norm regulating the conduct of the authority is content-dependent on the norm binding on the individual. The authority will not be able to impose a penalty on the individual if there has been no violation of the binding regulation. If the content of this primary norm is determined by taking into account statements formulated by non-state actors, they will also indirectly influence the shape of the norm binding the authority (see Sects. 2.2 and 5.1).

Secondly, the statements of a non-state actor may directly influence the norm of court. This influence is of a heterogeneous nature. In theory, the statements of a non-state actor could clarify the order for the imposition of a penalty in certain circumstances, performing binding acts of criminalisation. In practice, such a situation does not arise. The competence to criminalise behaviour remains in the sphere of the imperium. Delegations must therefore be regarded as its only source. As indicated above, situations of delegation of such powers to non-state actors are rare. The EU is one of the exceptions here, but it is not active in this area.

Much more often, non-state actors make statements that limit the discretion of the courts and restrict the scope of criminalisation. For example, they prohibit the criminalisation of certain behaviour (e.g. assembly, crossing border by the refugee) or by declaring certain forms of state reaction unacceptable (e.g. push backs—see Sect. 6.1). On the merits, these are primarily regulations defining the scope of human rights protection. Their source is both the judgments of international tribunals and the statements of other statutory bodies.[17] At the current stage of development of international law, it is this area that will most strongly limit the scope of the *ius puniendi*. State authorities obtain information on what categories of behaviour have to

---

[15] UN Human Rights Committee, General Comment No. 31 [80] Nature of the General Legal Obligation Imposed on States Parties to the Covenant, UN Doc. CCPR/C/21/Rev.1/Add.13 (26 May 2004), https://digitallibrary.un.org/record/533996. Document indicates: "The article 2, paragraph 1, obligations are binding on States [Parties] and do not, as such, have direct horizontal effect as a matter of international law".

[16] Österdahl (2015, p. 127).

[17] Ulfstein (2015, p. 250).

be permitted—as being under the protection of human rights. This may have the effect of narrowing the scope of criminalisation in the process of interpreting norms. To quote von Bogdandy and Goldmann: "If an activity of international institutions does not affect liberty or human rights significantly, it does not need to be conceptualized in a public law perspective".[18] This influence may take the form not only of restrictions, but also of an expansion of civil liberties.

This type of influence on the content of penal norms entails further complications. The regulations that make up the human rights system limit the discretion of the state. That is, they modify the norm that binds persons, acting as its public functionaries: police officers, customs officers, etc. (the norm of the individual).[19] The question arises whether the scope of the powers of these persons can be decoded using the regulations provided by the non-state actor. The answer is not obvious here, for two reasons. Firstly, what is happening here is not a limitation of criminalisation, but an extension of it. According to many legal systems, the actions of officers, taken in connection with their function, may constitute a criminal offence if they were taken in excess of their powers and thus led to damage.[20] An officer's conduct becomes unlawful precisely as a result of taking into account the statements made by non-state actors. Secondly, the addressee of this type of regulation is primarily the state and not the individual. Moreover, a police officer or a customs officer has limited possibilities to interpret binding international regulations. Within the hierarchical structures of the uniformed services, he or she remains bound by executive acts and often also by order.

Both of the above circumstances, however, do not constitute sufficient arguments to exclude the possibility of the regulation of non-state actors being invoked at all as elements of norms binding on officials. For the state is not an abstract entity, but is a form of organisation of power structures whose representatives are bound by international law precisely by virtue of their office. This position is widely represented

---

[18] Bogdandy and Goldmann (2008, p. 261).

[19] Pauwelyn et al. (2015, p. 70). Author says: "If citizen C fails to do x, then a certain legal official A is empowered$_1$ to impose a certain sanction y on C, and if A fails to impose y on C, then legal official B is empowered$_2$ to impose a certain sanction z on A".

[20] For example, according to the § 240 of the German Criminal Code in the version published on 13 November 1998 (Federal Law Gazette I, p. 3322), as last amended by Article 2 of the Act of 22 November 2021, Federal Law Gazette I, p. 4906 (StGB), https://www.gesetze-im-internet.de/englisch_stgb/. Accessed 20 September 2023.): "Coercion (Nötigung) (1) Whoever unlawfully, by force or threat of serious harm, compels a person to do, acquiesce to or refrain from an act incurs a penalty of imprisonment for a term not exceeding three years or a fine. (2) The act is unlawful if the use of force or the threat of harm is deemed reprehensible in respect of the desired objective. (3) The attempt is punishable. (4) In especially serious cases, the penalty is imprisonment for a term of between 6 months and 5 years. An especially serious case typically occurs where the offender". Act of 6 June 1997 The Polish Penal Code, Dz. U. 1997 Nr 88 poz. 553, with further amendments, https://www.imolin.org/doc/amlid/Poland_Penal_Code1.pdf. indicates in the Article 231 § 1: "A public official who, exceeding his/her powers or failing to fulfil his/her duties, acts to the detriment of public or private interest, shall be subject to imprisonment for up to 3 years". The scope of such duties may be defined also by the regulations of non-state actors.

in the doctrine in the case of the construction of crimes under international law.[21] There are no sufficient reasons to abandon this type of inference in the case of other regulations limiting the actions of state organs. If it can be established that the addressee of the regulation of the non-state actor was a specific public official, it should be included in the content of the norm of the individual binding upon him. For this purpose, it should be verified whether the considered statement of the non-state actor corresponds to the scope of duties incumbent upon the perpetrator. For while the prohibition to block certain demonstrations can be considered to be also addressed to a police officer, it is impossible to assume that he is bound by, for example, the recommendation to guarantee appropriate living conditions in a prison cell. A breach of such a norm may involve exceeding the powers of a public official, which in turn may constitute a criminal offence.

5.3 Self-contained and Interpretative Regulations of Non-state Actors

In order to correctly determine the impact of a given non-state actor regulation on the content of penal norms, it is necessary to determine whether it is of an intrinsic nature or whether it merely refers to other statements, being only an auxiliary source of law.

In the case of self-standing, the regulation determines its own content. Its effectiveness (its suitability to co-create a norm) is limited only by the extent of the competence of the non-state actor to establish it Examples include ISO standards or ICANN regulations. They do not refer to any specific provision of international law, but they have independent character. Of course, their interpretation does not take place in a vacuum, but the normative context here is dictated by the factual situation at hand rather than a strict normative connection.

In the case of regulations of an interpretative nature, the condition for deeming them to be binding is to show that they are consistent with the content of the regulations they interpret. By means of interpretation, the content of a treaty obligation incumbent on a state is modified here.[22] This category includes, first and foremost, theses contained in judgments of international tribunals and their justifications. Terms such as inhuman treatment[23] or genocide are developed in international law, with the

[21] Steer (2011, p. 295). In ICRC Commentary to Geneva Convention (II) we can read: "Official capacity, such as being a head of State or head of government, does not exempt a person from criminal responsibility for grave breaches, but may render such persons immune from proceedings before domestic courts on the basis of the existing state of international law". Convention (II) for the Amelioration of the Condition of Wounded, Sick and Shipwrecked Members of Armed Forces at Sea. Geneva, 12 August 1949. Commentary of 2017. Article 50: penal sanctions, https://ihl-databases.icrc.org/en/ihl-treaties/gcii-1949/article-50/commentary/2017.

[22] Fitzmaurice (2015, p. 199), Davies (2013).

[23] See *inter alia*: Prosecutor v. Zdravko Mucic aka "Pavo", Hazim Delic, Esad Landzo aka "Zenga", Zejnil Delalic (Trial Judgement), IT-96-21-T, ICTY, 16 November 1998, https://www.refworld.org/cases,ICTY,41482bde4.html; Prosecutor v. Dario Kordic, Mario Cerkez (Trial Judgement), IT-95-

involvement of the ICC, ICTY, ICTR or ECtHR.[24] As Steer indicates: "in the field of international criminal law (ICL), non-state actors play a key role not only as so-called subjects of the law, but more importantly as lawmakers in this nascent branch of international law".[25] Statements of such actors may, in a given context, play a key role in establishing the premise of criminal responsibility under national law. In certain situations, it is only by analysing them that it will be possible to determine what the torture referred to in the national criminalisation provision actually is. Domestic courts consider them as worthy taking into account in the interpretation process, as they refer to the same social issue. This is in fact an example of the use of systemic interpretation. However, these entities cannot practise legislation in the classic sense of the word.[26] They only have competence in the area of jurisdiction, not legislation. At the same time, however, states undertake to respect their judgments, which in practice means accepting their proposed interpretations as binding—on a similar basis to the case law of national higher courts.[27] Judicial statements become elements of penal norm (see Sect. 7.1). A similar assessment should be made of some of the regulations formulated by statutory bodies other than tribunals. Where they have not been given the authority to formulate legally binding statements (as EU bodies have), there their statements constitute only a general and abstract interpretation of the treaty (hard international law) provisions.[28] In this view, the activities of statutory bodies are similar to the functions performed by constitutional courts,[29] although their statements are not characterised by similar binding force. The HRC, for example, is seen in these terms, pointing out: "While the function of the Human Rights Committee in considering individual communications is not, as such, that of a judicial body, the views issued by the Committee under the Optional Protocol exhibit some important characteristics of a judicial decision".[30] These statements are not binding in the sense of a legal injunction. Their binding force is based on the strength of the authority of the entity itself or of the system to which it belongs (UN, EU, CE), which provide an argument for the state to agree to respect them (see Sect. 4.2). For example, the Views (Views) of the Human Rights Committee,

---

14/2-T, ICTY, 26 February 2001, https://www.refworld.org/cases,ICTY,41483e9be.html. In Delalic case ICTY provides the new element of definition: "serious attack on human dignity".

[24] Article 6 of the ICC Statute should be interpreted in connection with ICTY and ICTR decisions. See *inter alia*: Prosecutor v. Goran Jelisic (Trial Judgement), IT-95-10-T, ICTY, 14 December 1999, https://www.refworld.org/cases,ICTY,4147fe474.html; The Prosecutor v. Clément Kayishema and Obed Ruzindana (Trial Judgement), ICTR-95-1-T, ICTR, 21 May 1999, https://www.refworld.org/cases,ICTR,48abd5760.html; Schabas (2022, p. 120), Herik and Stahn (2012, p. 29).

[25] Steer (2011, p. 295).

[26] Leino (2015, p. 237).

[27] See inter alia: Harmsen (2007), Bjorge (2015, p. 223), Caligiuri and Napoletano (2010, p. 131).

[28] Ulfstein (2015, p. 253).

[29] Ibid., p. 253.

[30] UN Human Rights Committee, General comment no. 33, Obligations of States parties under the Optional Protocol to the International Covenant on Civil and Political Rights, 25 June 2009, CCPR/C/GC/33, https://documents-dds-ny.un.org/doc/UNDOC/GEN/G09/432/66/PDF/G0943266.pdf?OpenElement.

established under Article 28 of the ICCPR, are a widely respected source of interpretation of the Covenant.[31] The special case of regulations influencing the shape of the domestic interpretation is also Framework decisions of the EU.[32]

This raises the risk of an overly broad interpretation resulting in a broadening of the scope of the obligation assumed by the state. This is contrary to the principle of sovereignty. For this reason, the content of an interpretative regulation is determined not only by the wording of the treaty itself to which it refers, but also by specific interpretative directives.[33] International tribunals and statutory bodies as principle should not apply purposive and dynamic interpretation.[34] It does, however, happen in practice, often with the agreement of the states. For example in Tyrer case the ECtHR indicated that: "the Convention is a living instrument which, as the Commission rightly stressed, must be interpreted in the light of present-day conditions".[35] It should be emphasised that the Court has here taken as a benchmark the change in the standard of protection resulting from the internal practice of the States Parties.[36] Other example of this is the HRC's recognition that an element of the right to life is the right to housing, nutrition and health.[37]

Going beyond the rules of interpretation permissible in this area is an argument for disregarding the non-state actor's statement in question when interpreting the penal norm.

The categories of regulations described above interact with each other, either complementing or conflicting in content. In order to interpret them together, it is necessary to determine the concurrence of regulations occurring in this context.

References

Beijer M (2017) Limits of fundamental rights protection by the EU: the scope for the development of positive obligations. Intersentia, Cambridge, Antwerp, Portland

Bjorge E (2015) Domestic application of the ECHR: courts as faithful trustees. Oxford University Press, Oxford

Bogdandy AV, Venzke I (2012) Beyond dispute: international judicial institutions as lawmakers. In: Bogdandy AV, Venzke I (eds) International judicial Lawmaking: on public authority and democratic legitimation in global governance. Springer, Heidelberg

Brolmann C, Radi Y (2016) Research handbook on the theory and practice of international Lawmaking. Edward Elgar Publishing, Cheltenham, Northhampton, Cheltenham

---

[31] Ulfstein (2015, p. 253).

[32] Satzger (2017, p. 123); Criminal proceedings against Maria Pupino, Case C-105/03, European Court Reports 2005 I-05285.

[33] Ulfstein (2015, p. 256).

[34] Ibid., p. 257.

[35] Tyrer v. the United Kingdom (application No. 5856/72), https://hudoc.echr.coe.int/fre#{%22itemid%22:[%22001-57587%22]}.

[36] Beijer (2017, p. 29).

[37] Ulfstein (2015, p. 257), Khaliq and Churchill (2012, p. 202).

Caligiuri A, Napoletano N (2010) The application of the ECHR in the domestic systems. Ital Yearb Int Law Online 20:125–159. https://doi.org/10.1163/22116133-90000173
Crawford J (2019) Brownlie's principles of public international law, 9th edn. Oxford University Press, Oxford, New York
Creutz K (2015) International responsibility and problematic law-making. In: Liivoja R, Petman J (eds) International law-making: essays in honour of Jan Klabbers, 1st edn. Routledge, Abingdon, Oxon
d'Aspremont J (2011) Non-state actors in international law: oscillating between concepts and dynamics. In: d'Aspremont J (ed) Participants in the international legal system: multiple perspectives on non-state actors in international law. Routledge, London
d'Aspremont J (2011) The politics of deformalization in international law. Goettingen J Int Law. https://doi.org/10.3249/1868-1581-3-2-ASPREMONT
Davies P (2013) Non-compliance—a pivotal or secondary function of CoP governance? Int Community Law Rev 15:77–101. https://doi.org/10.1163/18719732-12341243
Fitzmaurice M (2015) Law-making and international environmental law. In: Liivoja R, Petman J (eds) International law-making: essays in honour of Jan Klabbers, 1st edn. Routledge, Abingdon, Oxon
Fontanelli F (2011) ISO and Codex Standards and international trade law: what gets said is not what's heard. Int Comp Law Q 60:895–932. https://doi.org/10.1017/S0020589311000431
Geiger R (2015) Framework, goals and bases of the EU. In: Geiger R, Khan D-E, Kotzur M (eds) European Union treaties: a commentary: treaty on European Union—treaty on the functioning of the European Union—charter of fundamental rights of the European Union. München, Oxford
Harmsen R (2007) The European Court of human rights as a "constitutional court". In: Morison J, McEvoy K, Anthony G (eds) Judges, transition, and human rights, 1st edn. Oxford University Press, Oxford, New York
Herik L van den, Stahn C (2012) 'Fragmentation', diversification and '3D' legal pluralism: international criminal law as the jack-in-the-box? In: Herik L van den, Stahn C (eds) The diversification and fragmentation of international criminal law. Brill Nijhoff, Leiden, Boston
Hernandez G (2016) International judicial lawmaking. In: Brölmann C, Radi Y (eds) Research handbook on the theory and practice of international Lawmaking. Edward Elgar Publishing, Cheltenham
Khaliq U, Churchill R (2012) The protection of economic and social rights: a particular challenge? In: Keller H, Ulfstein G (eds) UN human rights treaty bodies: law and legitimacy. Cambridge University Press, Cambridge, New York
Koskenniemi M (2015) Declaratory legislation. In: Liivoja R, Petman J (eds) International law-making: essays in honour of Jan Klabbers, 1st edn. Routledge, Abingdon, Oxon
Kratochwil F (2015) Legalism and the 'dark' side of global governance. In: Liivoja R, Petman J (eds) International law-making: essays in honour of Jan Klabbers, 1st edn. Routledge, Abingdon, Oxon
Leino P (2015) 'In principle the full review'. What justice for Mr Kadi? In: Liivoja R, Petman J (eds) International law-making: essays in honour of Jan Klabbers, 1st edn. Routledge, Abingdon, Oxon
Österdahl I (2015) (International) Law! In: Liivoja R, Petman J (eds) International law-making: essays in honour of Jan Klabbers, 1st edn. Routledge, Abingdon, Oxon
Pauwelyn J, Wessel RA, Wouters J (2015) Informal international law as presumptive law. In: Liivoja R, Petman J (eds) international law-making: essays in honour of Jan Klabbers, 1st edn. Routledge, Abingdon, Oxon
Satzger H (2017) International and European criminal law, 2nd edn. C.H. Beck, München, Oxford, Baden-Baden
Schabas WA (2022) Art. 6. In: Ambos K (ed) Rome statute of the international criminal court: article-by-article commentary, 4th edn. Beck/Hart, München, Oxford, Baden-Baden

Steer C (2011) Non-state actors in international criminal law. In: d'Aspremont J (ed) Participants in the international legal system: multiple perspectives on non-state actors in international law. Routledge, London

Ulfstein G (2015) Law-making by human rights treaty bodies. In: Liivoja R, Petman J (eds) International law-making: essays in honour of Jan Klabbers, 1st edn. Routledge, Abingdon, Oxon

von Bogdandy A, Goldmann M (2008) The exercise of international public authority through national policy assessment: The OECD's PISA policy as a paradigm for a new international standard instrument. Int Organ Law Rev 5:241–298. https://doi.org/10.1163/157237408X412907

Chapter 6
Conflict of Regulations-Elements of Norms

Abstract Particular regulations (potentially—elements of the norm) may be in conflict with each other. In such a situation, it will be necessary to refer to the conflict rules, which are specifically shaped in the case of international law. This chapter focusses on the practical application of the conflict rules in the case of combined interpretation of national and international law.

Keywords Conflict of regulations · Conflict rules · *Lex specialis* · *Lex superior* · International law

In the process of determining the content of penal norms, regulations of various origins are used. They are all subject to a cumulative interpretation, influencing each other. In practice, however, it may happen that there are irremediable discrepancies between them. This raises the question of how to resolve overlaps when the same issue is regulated by several normative statements in conflict with each other. When analysing the problem from the perspective of regulations formulated by non-state actors, the following points should be noted.

Firstly, the particular regulations, formulated by the non-state actor, come from different actors, which makes it considerably difficult to sort them out within the framework of the classical conflict rules. The phenomena of defragmentation[1] and constitutionalisation[2] directly impinge in this respect on the method of interpreting penal norms using the statements of non-state actors. The multiplicity of law-making centres (the UN, the EU, the Council of Europe, the OECD, the IOC) significantly hinders any movement within the hierarchy of regulations considered by the state. Establishing temporal succession is also problematic.

[1] On defragmentation see *inter alia*: Koskenniemi (2006), Herik and Stahn (2012), Koskenniemi (2014).

[2] On constitutionalisation see *inter alia*: Klabbers et al. (2011).

D. Zając, *Non-state Actors Law-making and Domestic Criminal Law*,
SpringerBriefs in Law, https://doi.org/10.1007/978-3-031-47870-3_6

Secondly, such a concurrence of regulation will always be decided *in concreto*.[3] The lack of a hierarchical structure in the relationship between national and international law makes it impossible to formulate strict and universal interpretative directives in this respect.[4] The concurrence must be resolved by the national court. It is the latter that is responsible for the final determination of the content of the norm, in accordance with the principle of *iura novit curia*.

Thirdly, practical problems arise only in situations of conflicting regulations, not the mere fact of their concurrence.[5] Where the same issue is regulated by multiple regulations in ways that are reconcilable at the level of content, there will be no interpretative problem at all. From the perspective of sentencing criteria, it is crucial to determine how to deal with statements between which there is a conflict (e.g. an order to impose a sentence of life imprisonment without parole and a prohibition to impose such a penalty).

Fourthly, it may happen that a regulation by a non-state actor addresses the same issue as a national regulation (another international regulation) but its addressee is not one of the addressees of the penal norms. Let us assume that the Commission on Narcotic Drugs of the UN has supplemented the list of prohibited substances with new drugs, but at the national level this has not been reflected in the content of the law (e.g. as a law or regulation). In this situation, the individual is not bound by the content of the updated list, as he or she is not the addressee (see Sect. 4.1). The statement of the Commission will not be able to constitute an element of the norm at all. The situation outlined here is an example of an apparent concurrence. There is no competition of normative statements at all, due to the divergence of their addressees.

Fifthly, a conflict occurs where two regulations compete for the status of the same element of a norm (prohibition/order, regulation clarifies its scope, prerequisites for punishment, etc.—see Sect. 7.1, 7.2 and 7.3). For example, the treatment of financial secrecy, to which the prohibition/order with a penalty applies, will be regulated simultaneously by the MAR Regulation and a non-repealed national law. It is not a conflict if there is a contentual overlap between the scope of the prohibition/order and the regulation that clarifies it.

The conflict here relates to regulations that could potentially become elements of the norm if they are considered "stronger". The entity interpreting the norm must resolve the conflict thus outlined by referring to three interpretative rules: *lex specialis*, *lex superior* and *lex posterior*. These are recognised both at the level of national systems and on the basis of international law. From the perspective of the present study, it is mainly the latter perspective that is of interest. The manner in which concurrences between international law and domestic law are resolved depends on the internal structure of the sources of law adopted by the state in question.

---

[3] Herik and Stahn (2012, p. 25).

[4] Klabbers et al. (2011, p. 32), Koskenniemi (2006, p. 47).

[5] See *inter alia* Vranes (2006, p. 395), Ferguson (2018, p. 51).

6.1 Conflict of Regulations from Perspective of Domestic Legal System

An in-depth comparative legal analysis of methods of resolving regulation's conflicts within domestic law is beyond the scope of this study. However, two points should be noted.

Firstly, some legal systems include specific types of international law acts in the internal structure of the sources of law. For example, Article 94 of The Constitution of the Kingdom of the Netherlands 2002 provides that: "Statutory regulations in force within the Kingdom shall not be applicable if such application is in conflict with provisions of treaties that are binding on all persons or of resolutions by international institutions".[6] The normative content of the acts in question is determined in practice by the statements of the actors, constituting the non-state actor. Some of them may clarify the content of international treaties (e.g. judgments of the ECtHR), the others are issued by virtue of delegation (e.g. EU regulations—see Sect. 3.1).[7] Acts of this type are often considered to be more important sources of internal law than acts of national parliaments. If a non-state actor's regulation constitutes a binding interpretation of a treaty or an act issued pursuant to a delegation, it will acquire the same position in the hierarchy of sources of internal law as a treaty. Where it is possible to establish such a hierarchical relationship, it may provide the basis for conflict resolution in accordance with the *lex superior principle*[8]. Depending on the shape of the national legal system, such a conflict may be resolved through interpretation, by the domestic court, or through a review similar to constitutional control mechanisms.

Secondly, statements by non-state actors are often categorised as soft law—dispositions without strict legal effect.[9] In this view, they constitute a quasi-source of law,

---

[6] The Constitution of the Kingdom of the Netherlands 2002, translation: rechtspraak.nl/SiteCollectionDocuments/Constitution-NL.pdf. Similar solution provides the Article 91 of the Constitution of the Republic of Poland of 2 April 1997, as published in Dziennik Ustaw No. 78, item 483, https://www.sejm.gov.pl/prawo/konst/angielski/kon1.htm, which stipulates: "1. After promulgation thereof in the Journal of Laws of the Republic of Poland (Dziennik Ustaw), a ratified international agreement shall constitute part of the domestic legal order and shall be applied directly, unless its application depends on the enactment of a statute. 2. An international agreement ratified upon prior consent granted by statute shall have precedence over statutes if such an agreement cannot be reconciled with the provisions of such statutes. 3. If an agreement, ratified by the Republic of Poland, establishing an international organization so provides, the laws established by it shall be applied directly and have precedence in the event of a conflict of laws".

[7] Satzger (2017, p. 55).

[8] Ibid., p. 109.

[9] On idea of soft law see *inter alia*: Hage (2018, p. 19). The Author indicates: "Phenomena that are labeled as 'soft law' are omnipresent. The expression 'soft law' is often used to refer to rules based on quasi-legal instruments, which lack legally 'binding force', whatever that may be, or whose binding force is somewhat weaker than the binding force of traditional law. Examples include the UN Declaration of Human Rights, recommendations in the law of the European Union, tax resolutions, published governmental policies, self-regulation in particular branches of society, codes of conduct for companies and governmental organizations, restatements of the common law, and case law in

which should give way to national laws in the event of conflict. For example, part of the regulation of non-state actors binds by virtue of the consent of the individual who aligns his or her conduct with the international standard or as a transfer of knowledge to the level of norms. However, the state has the right to formulate binding statements, limiting the scope of freedom of action, and to carry out its own transfer, taking into account, for example, the acceptability of risk. If, in a given situation, the state introduces a different legal standard, the court must consider it as binding in the process of decoding the norm (see Sect. 3.3).

6.2 Conflict of Regulations at the Level of International Law

In practice, it may be the case that conflicts between regulations formulated by non-state actors will have to be resolved at the level of international law, taking into account the specificities of this branch of law. In certain situations, it will be necessary to take into account, for example, the hierarchy of acts inherent only in international law or the predominant nature of certain regimes. These considerations are not reflected in national conflict of laws rules.

6.2.1 *Lex Specialis Principle in International Law*

In accordance with the principle of *lex specialis*, the content of the penal norm should be determined on the basis of that regulation which is deemed to be special in relation to the general one.[10] It is assumed that a regulation which is *lex specialis* is characterised by greater precision and constitutes a more effective tool for regulating the behaviour of its addressees.[11] The principle of *lex specialis* has not been codified in Treaty Law, but its binding force in the area of international law is generally accepted by doctrine and jurisprudence.[12]

---

the civil law tradition. Despite this ubiquity of soft law—which, by the way, does not always go by that name—the precise nature of soft law is not yet clear, and it is possible that there is more than one kind of soft law".

[10] Orakhelashvili (2008, p. 371).

[11] Koskenniemi (2006, p. 36).

[12] Zob. m.in. Yankov v. Bulgaria, 39084/97, Judgment of 11 December 2003, ECHR 2003-XII, https://hudoc.echr.coe.int/eng#{%22appno%22:[%2239084/97%22],%22itemid%22:[%22001-61539%22]}; Iran-United States Claims Tribunal, Case No. A/2, Iran v. US C.T.R. vol 1, 1981–1982; Koskenniemi (2006, p. 39); Military and Paramilitary Activities in and against Nicaragua (Nicaragua v. United States of America). Merits, Judgment. I.C.J. Reports 1986, p. 14, https://www.icj-cij.org/public/files/case-related/70/070-19860627-JUD-01-00-EN.pdf. In the judgment, the ICJ pointed out that: "In general, treaty rules being *lex specialis*, it would not be appropriate

An effective application of the *lex specialis* as a conflict rule will occur where the specific law introduces a solution that is different in content, specifying an exception to the general regulation. The ILC points out that: "For the lex specialis principle to apply it is not enough that the same subject matter is dealt with by two provisions; there must be some actual inconsistency between them, or else a discernible intention that one provision is to exclude the other. Thus, the question is essentially one of interpretation".[13] An example is the international law of war, which lowers the standard of protection of human life during armed conflict.[14]

In practice, determining which of the converging regulations constitutes a lex specialis can pose significant difficulties. The rule in question is relational in nature: it is not possible to confer lex specialis status on a general level. The same regulation may be considered special in one setting and general in another.[15] The feature of being special may result from the reference of a given regulation to specific factual situations, e.g. determining the content of an international obligation in the reality of a state of emergency.[16] The principle itself escapes strict definitions, there is no way to codify it effectively.[17]

Despite such a fluid nature of the lex specialis principle, certain limitation points can be identified, limiting the scope of its application. Certainly, the lex specialis principle cannot lead to a derogation of *ius cogens* regulations.[18] Some representatives of the doctrine are likewise inclined to treat the regulations referred to in Article 103 of the UN Charter in the same way.[19] The regulations that make up the human rights regime are also given special protection from derogation.[20] *Lex specialis* principle allows for the resolution of both concurrences within a single system (e.g. UN, EU, Council of Europe[21]) and external concurrences. In the case of internal concurrences, it should be used taking into account the internal hierarchy of sources of law inherent

that a State should bring a claim based on a customary-law rule if it has by treaty already provided means for settlement of a such a claim".

[13] Draft articles on Responsibility of States for Internationally Wrongful Acts, with commentaries, Text adopted by the International Law Commission at its fifty-third session, in 2001, and submitted to the General Assembly as a part of the Commission's report covering the work of that session (A/56/10), https://legal.un.org/ilc/texts/instruments/english/commentaries/9_6_2001.pdf, p. 140.

[14] Legality of the Threat or Use of Nuclear Weapons, Advisory Opinion, I.C.J. Reports 1996, p. 226, https://www.icj-cij.org/sites/default/files/case-related/95/095-19960708-ADV-01-00-EN.pdf. The ICJ ruling indicated: "The test of what is an arbitrary deprivation of life, however, then falls to be determined by the applicable lex specialis, namely, the law applicable in armed conflict which is designed to regulate the conduct of hostilities. Thus whether a particular loss of life, through the use of a certain weapon in warfare, is to be considered an arbitrary deprivation of life contrary to Article 6 of the Covenant, can only be decided by reference to the law applicable in armed conflict and not deduced from the terms of the Covenant itself".

[15] Koskenniemi (2006, p. 61).

[16] Ibid., p. 57.

[17] Ibid., p. 64.

[18] Ibid., p. 131.

[19] Ibid., p. 59.

[20] Ibid., p. 59.

[21] Ibid., p. 41.

in the system in question.[22] It also makes it possible to resolve issues that remain at the intersection of regimes (for example, human rights regime and anti-terrorist regulations).

6.2.2 Lex Posterior Principle in International Law

The lex posterior principle refers to the concurrence of regulations in terms of time. It constitutes a general principle recognised by civilised nations.[23] Its essence boils down to the recognition that the formulation of a new regulation relating to the same subject-matter excludes the effectiveness of an obligation previously binding in this respect. Re-regulation of the same issue will, in principle, result from the need to adapt the content of the law to the changing socio-political environment. For this reason, the newer regulation should be regarded as better—and as such it should supersede the earlier regulation. The principle of lex posterior functions in a manner similar to lex specialis, although it adopts a different criterion of derogation. Invoking it may not lead to the exclusion of the effectiveness of regulations of *ius cogens* nature or regulations referred to in Article 103 of the Charter of the United Nations.[24]

The applicability of the lex posterior principle in resolving conflicts between non-state actors' regulations is severely limited. Determining the relation of temporal succession requires the juxtaposition of two statements, concerning the same issue and coming from the same legislative entity. In practice, this will very often involve a formal derogation of the earlier regulation. For example, a decision of the Commission on Narcotic Drugs of 2 December 2020[25] moved cannabis plant (marijuana) from class IV to class I narcotic substances, according to the lists annexed to the UN drug conventions. Formal derogation is also taking place in subsequent EU legislative acts. The new regulation formulated by the non-state actor supersedes the earlier regulation.

The *lex posterior* principle suffers further complications when set in the context of penal norms. In practice, it may turn out that, although a given regulation has been replaced by a more recent one, due to the binding force of the domestic system of criminal law, the court is bound by the lex retro non agit principle. In a specific case it may turn out that in order to decode the content of the norm, it will be necessary to take into account the content of the law binding at the moment of committing the act by the perpetrator.

---

[22] Ibid., p. 43.

[23] Ibid., p. 117.

[24] Ibid., p. 131.

[25] Press Statement—2 December 2020, CND votes on recommendations for cannabis and cannabis-related substances, https://www.unodc.org/documents/commissions/CND/CND_Sessions/CND_63Reconvened/Press_statement_CND_2_December.pdf. "The Commission decided by 27 votes to 25 and with one abstention to follow this recommendation. Cannabis and cannabis resin will accordingly be deleted from Schedule IV of the 1961 Convention. They remain in Schedule I of the 1961 Convention and thus remain subject to all levels of control of the 1961 Convention".

6.2.3 Lex Superior Principle in International Law

The harmonisation of inconsistencies between similar regulations based on the principle of lex superior is a familiar process in national law systems. However, while in national laws this operation is carried out within a single legal system, based—in principle—on the same set of constitutional (superior) norms, in the case of international law there is no common denominator to which one can refer in the process of exegesis.[26] However, this does not mean that there are no hierarchical links.

Firstly, although it is not possible to refer to a specific act of constitutional rank, there are peremptory regulations in the area of international law. As indicated in the ILC Report: "There has never been any doubt about the fact that some considerations in the international world are more important than others, and must be legally recognized as such".[27] The existence of this type of regulation is also confirmed by the jurisprudence of international tribunals.[28] In this respect, two categories of international law regulations can be distinguished: ius cogens regulations and provisions contained in the UN Charter.[29] From the perspective of the activity of non-state actors, the latter category is crucial. According to the Article 103 of the Charter[30]: " In the event of a conflict between the obligations of the Members of the United Nations under the present Charter and their obligations under any other international agreement, their obligations under the present Charter shall prevail". Such a provision, in fact, introduces a presumption of the predominant character of the obligations, as formulated in the Charter, and in virtually universal terms.[31] They are characterised by priority in application.[32] To fully perceive the normative significance of Article 103 of the UN Charter, it is necessary to relate it to the content of the document itself. It does not consist only of directives of conduct, precisely describing how States Parties should behave. Among other things, the UN Charter contains a cross-referencing provision. The Article 25 of the UN Charter states that: "The Members of the United Nations agree to accept and carry out the decisions of the Security Council in accordance with the present Charter". A combined analysis of both regulations leads to the conclusion that the regulations adopted by the UN Security Council will also take priority.[33] However, even these give way to ius cogens regulations. The assessment of the legality of UNSC resolutions should be made: "in the light of the

---

[26] Klabbers et al. (2011, p. 59), Koskenniemi (2006, p. 166).

[27] Koskenniemi (2006, p. 167).

[28] Corfu Channel case (the United Kingdom v. Albania) I.C.J. Reports 1949, p. 22; Legality of the Threat or Use of Nuclear Weapons, Advisory Opinion, I.C.J. Reports 1996, p. 226, https://www.icj-cij.org/sites/default/files/case-related/95/095-19960708-ADV-01-00-EN.pdf, p. 257. *The Corfu case* used the phrase: "general and well-recognized principles, namely: elementary considerations of humanity".

[29] Klabbers et al. (2011, p. 16), Koskenniemi (2006, p. 183).

[30] Koskenniemi (2006, p. 168).

[31] Liivoja (2008, p. 583), Kitharidis (2016, p. 112).

[32] Koskenniemi (2006, p. 172).

[33] Ibid., p. 169.

higher rules of international law falling within the ambit of jus *cogens*, in particular the mandatory prescriptions concerning the universal protection of the rights of the human person".[34]

Secondly, the identification of a specific hierarchy of sources of law is possible within the systems themselves, which are themselves hierarchical in nature. The law created within the UN or the EU refers in its content to foundation acts: UN Charter or TFEU. Implementing acts and statements of a technical nature are often clarifications of higher order acts. In the event of conflict, however, they must give way to higher order acts.

6.3 Case Study: Al-Jedda and Kadi

In practice, the application of the above conflict of laws rules may pose significant problems. This is illustrated by the example of the conflict between anti-terrorist and human rights regulations. This leads to a kind of clinch. On the one hand, the human rights protection regime is treated holistically as *lex specialis*.[35] This also applies to statements by international tribunals, e.g. the ECHR. On the other hand, anti-terrorism regulations are sometimes formulated within the framework of UNSC Resolutions, on the basis of Chapter VII of the UN Charter. This, in turn, gives them a higher place in the hierarchy of legislation, on the basis of Article 103 of the Charter. A regulation that is considered "stronger" will be able to become an element of the penal norm, and thus constitute one of the criteria for assigning possible criminal liability.

To set the above in the context of specific jurisprudential problems, we consider the case of Al-Jedda and Kadi.

The case of Al-Jedda v. Secretary of State for Defence[36] has been considered by the UK courts, including the House of Lords,[37] and, subsequently, by the ECtHR. Al-Jedda was a British citizen and an Iraqi citizen, interned for 10 months without charge—on suspicion of a terrorist offence. Prima facie this was a breach of the UK's human rights standard of protection, referring to the ECHR. In the ruling, however, the British court referred to the need to have regard to Security Council

[34] Case T-306/01, Ahmed Ali Yusuf and Al Barakaat International Foundation v. Council of the European Union and Commission of the European Communities, https://curia.europa.eu/juris/showPdf.jsf?text=&docid=59905&pageIndex=0&doclang=en&mode=lst&dir=&occ=first&part=1&cid=1431524.

[35] Simma and Pulkowski (2006, p. 511).

[36] Al-Jedda v. Secretary of State for Defence, [2010] EWCA Civ 758, United Kingdom: Court of Appeal (England and Wales), 8 July 2010, https://www.casemine.com/judgement/uk/5a8ff71360d03e7f57ea728c.

[37] R (on the application of Al-Jedda) (FC) (Appellant) v Secretary of State for Defence (Respondent) [2007] UKHL 58, [2007] UKHL 58, United Kingdom: House of Lords (Judicial Committee), 12 December 2007, https://publications.parliament.uk/pa/ld200708/ldjudgmt/jd071212/jedda-1.htm; Messineo (2009).

Resolution 1511 (and the subsequent United Nations Security Council Resolution 1546), which indicated that Multinational Force: "shall have the authority to take all necessary measures to contribute to the maintenance of security and stability in Iraq in accordance with the letters annexed to this Resolution expressing, inter alia, the Iraqi request for the continued presence of the Multinational Force and setting out its tasks, including by preventing and deterring terrorism".[38] The British authorities considered the internment of suspects as one form of "necessary measures". In justifying the House of Lords' decision, Lord Bingham pointed out: "Thus there is a clash between on the one hand a power or duty to detain exercisable on the express authority of the Security Council and, on the other, a fundamental human right which the UK has undertaken to secure to those (like the appellant) within its jurisdiction. How are these to be reconciled? There is in my opinion only one way in which they can be reconciled: by ruling that the UK may lawfully, where it is necessary for imperative reasons of security, exercise the power to detain authorised by UNSCR 1546 and successive resolutions, but must ensure that the detainee's rights under Article 5 are not infringed to any greater extent than is inherent in such detention".[39] By recognising the supremacy of the Resolution, the British judiciary actually lowered the national standard of human rights protection by invoking the principle of lex superior. The regulation, issued by a non-state actor, led to a modification of the rules of conduct binding on British officers.

The above ruling was subsequently challenged before the ECtHR.[40] The Court agreed in principle with the reasoning presented by the British judiciary, referring to the special place of the acts referred to in Article 103 of the UN Charter. At the same time, however, it carried out the reasoning in concreto, relating it to a concretised obligation of the State. The judgment pointed out: "Article 103 of the Charter of the United Nations provides that the obligations of the members of the United Nations under the Charter shall prevail in the event of a conflict with obligations under any other international agreement. Before it can consider whether Article 103 had any application in the present case, the Court must determine whether there was a conflict between the United Kingdom's obligations under United Nations Security Council Resolution 1546 and its obligations under Article 5 § 1 of the Convention. In other words, the key question is whether Resolution 1546 placed the United Kingdom under an obligation to hold the applicant in internment". The question thus posed was answered in the negative. In the grounds for the judgment, it was pointed out: "The Court does not consider that the language used in this Resolution indicates unambiguously that the Security Council intended to place member States within

[38] UN Security Council, Security Council resolution 1546 (2004) [on formation of a sovereign Interim Government of Iraq], 8 June 2004, S/RES/1546 (2004), https://digitallibrary.un.org/record/523025/files/S_RES_1546%282004%29-EN.pdf?ln=en.

[39] R (on the application of Al-Jedda) (FC) (Appellant) v Secretary of State for Defence (Respondent) [2007] UKHL 58, [2007] UKHL 58, United Kingdom: House of Lords (Judicial Committee), 12 December 2007, https://publications.parliament.uk/pa/ld200708/ldjudgmt/jd071212/jedda-1.htm.

[40] Al-Jedda v. United Kingdom, Application no. 27021/08, Council of Europe: European Court of Human Rights, 7 July 2011, https://hudoc.echr.coe.int/fre#{%22itemid%22:[%22001-105612%22]}..

the Multinational Force under an obligation to use measures of indefinite internment without charge and without judicial guarantees, in breach of their undertakings under international human rights instruments including the Convention. Internment is not explicitly referred to in the Resolution". According to the ECtHR, there was no conflict between the Resolution and the ECHR at all in the Al-Jedda case, and the conflict was therefore apparent. The Court's statement, also a manifestation of non-actor law-making, led to a narrowing of the disposition flowing from the Security Council Resolution.

The same concurrence of regulations was therefore decided differently by the British courts and the ECtHR. Without conducting an in-depth analysis of the conclusions presented, it should be noted that it was crucial here to determine the meaning of the term "necessary measures". According to the British courts, internment was such a necessary measure—the mildest measure that could be taken to fulfil the resolution. In the view of the ECtHR—there were other effective methods of achieving the objectives set by the UNSC. Therefore, it was not so much the application of the conflict of laws rules that proved problematic, but the determination of the normative meaning of the statement, as formulated by the non-state actor (UNSC). The lack of precision allowed the ECtHR to assume that the Resolution did not require the use of internment. At the same time, however, the ECtHR did not indicate what other measures, in the circumstances of the case at hand, were to be considered sufficient to achieve the objectives of the proceedings.

The second case commented on was the blocking of funds of those suspected of having links to al-Qaeda—under Security Council Resolution 1267.[41] The list of persons sanctioned included Yassin Kadi, who is a Saudi businessman—his name was mentioned in the Sanctions Committee's decision of 19 October 2001. The implementation of the instruments described in the Resolution also took place within the framework of EU (then European Communities) law. Regulation EC No 467/2001 of 6 March 2001 contained an Annex which specified the list of persons subject to sanctions. Annex I to Regulation 467/2001 contains a list of persons, entities and organisations whose funds and other financial resources were subject to a freeze. Yassin Kadi was included in the list by Commission Regulation (EC) No. 2062/2001 of 19 October 2001. This decision was challenged by him before the ECJ.[42] The Court of First Instance of the European Communities dismissed his complaint.[43] However,

---

[41] UN Security Council, Security Council resolution 1267 (1999) [Afghanistan], 15 October 1999, S/RES/1267 (1999), https://documents-dds-ny.un.org/doc/UNDOC/GEN/N99/300/44/PDF/N9930044.pdf?OpenElement.

[42] The case has been widely analysed in the literature. See *inter alia*: Leino (2015, p. 226). An analogous problem arose, inter alia, on the grounds of the Case T-318/01 Othman v. Council and Commission [2009] ECR II-1627, https://curia.europa.eu/juris/document/document.jsf?text=&docid=75450&pageIndex=0&doclang=EN&mode=req&dir=&occ=first&part=1&cid=1436698.

[43] The judgments of the Court of First Instance of the European Communities of 21 September 2005 in Case T-315/01 Kadi v Council and Commission [2005] ECR II-3649, https://curia.europa.eu/juris/showPdf.jsf?text=&docid=59906&pageIndex=0&doclang=en&mode=lst&dir=&occ=first&part=1&cid=1436698.

the judgment was overturned by a decision of the Grand Chamber.[44] Without quoting the detailed reasoning of the Grand Appellate Judgement here, it is worth quoting two passages from it. Firstly, the ECJ pointed out that: "by virtue of that provision, supposing it to be applicable to the Charter of the United Nations, the latter would have primacy over acts of secondary Community law (see, to that effect, Case C-308/06 Intertanko and Others [2008] ECR I-0000, paragraph 42 and case-law cited). That primacy at the level of Community law would not, however, extend to primary law, in particular to the general principles of which fundamental rights form part". Here, in fact, the primacy of the provisions of the UNSC was challenged. This, in turn, opened the way for a review of the EC Council Regulation, which is in fact a kind of implementing act of the UNSC Resolution. Indeed, it was further pointed out: "It follows from the foregoing that the Community judicature must, in accordance with the powers conferred on it by the EC Treaty, ensure the review, in principle the full review, of the lawfulness of all Community acts in the light of the fundamental rights forming an integral part of the general principles of Community law, including review of Community measures which, like the contested regulation, are designed to give effect to the resolutions adopted by the Security Council under Chapter VII of the Charter of the United Nations". The right to judicial review of the decisions of state authorities as well as the related procedural safeguards was considered here to take precedence over the content of the EC Council Regulation implementing the Resolution.

Looking at the above ruling through the prism of the conflict principles, two issues appear to be relevant. First, the ECJ did not recognise the primacy of the UNSC Resolution, which prima facie stood in opposition to the principle of *lex superior*. Secondly, the ECJ gave primacy to the regulations that make up the human rights regime, which, as already indicated, is seen as a *lex specialis* regime.

The analysis of the two cases shows that the practice of applying the conflict rules is strongly flexible. At the *in concreto* level, where there is a real possibility of judicial review, there the regulations that make up the human rights protection system are given priority. This applies in particular to EU states bound by the ECHR. The *lex superior* principle is bypassed or ignored in the process of analysis. Consequently, it can be hypothesised that in the event of a conflict between non-state actor regulation and human rights, it is the latter that should shape the state official's conduct. This is all the more important since authorities, in exercising their authority over an individual, must act within the limits and on the basis of the law. A breach of the laws that bind them may result in criminal liability—especially if it involves causing concrete harm (see Sect. 4.2).

---

[44] Judgment of the Court (Grand Chamber) of 3 September 2008, Yassin Abdullah Kadi and Al Barakaat International Foundation v Council of the European Union and Commission of the European Communities, ECLI:EU:C:2008:461, https://curia.europa.eu/juris/document/document.jsf?text=&docid=67611&pageIndex=0&doclang=en&mode=req&dir=&occ=first&part=1&cid=1439152.

References

Ferguson R (2018) Conflict of norms in international law: theories and practice. In: The right to food and the world trade organization's rules on agriculture: conflicting, compatible, or complementary? Brill Nijhoff, Leiden, Boston

Hage J (2018) What is legal validity? Lessons from soft law. In: Westerman P, Hage J, Kirste S, Mackor AR (eds) Legal validity and soft law. New York

Herik L van den, Stahn C (2012) 'Fragmentation', diversification and '3D' legal pluralism: international criminal law as the jack-in-the-box? In: Herik L van den, Stahn C (eds) The diversification and fragmentation of international criminal law. Brill Nijhoff, Leiden, Boston

Kitharidis S (2016) The power of Article 103 of the un charter on treaty obligations: can the security council authorise non-compliance of human rights treaty obligations in United Nations peacekeeping operations? J Int Peacekeep 20:111–131. https://doi.org/10.1163/18754112-02001008

Klabbers J, Peters A, Ulfstein G (2011) The constitutionalization of international law. Oxford University Press, Oxford, New York

Koskenniemi M (2006) Fragmentation of international law: difficulties arising from the diversification and expansion of international law: report of the Study Group of the International Law Commission, A/CN.4/L.682/Add.1., 2 May 2006. https://digitallibrary.un.org/record/574816/files/A_CN.4_L.682_Add.1-EN.pdf?ln=en

Koskenniemi M (2014) Fragmentation of international law: difficulties arising from the diversification and expansion of international law. Yearb Int Law Comm 2006, vol II, part 2. https://doi.org/10.18356/25997571-en

Leino P (2015) 'In principle the full review'. What justice for Mr Kadi? In: Liivoja R, Petman J (eds) International law-making: essays in honour of Jan Klabbers, 1st edn. Routledge, Abingdon, Oxon

Liivoja R (2008) The scope of the supremacy clause of the United Nations charter. Int Comp Law Q 57:583–612

Messineo F (2009) The house of lords in Al-Jedda and public international law: attribution of conduct to un-authorized forces and the power of the security council to displace human rights. Neth Int Law Rev 56:35–62. https://doi.org/10.1017/S0165070X09000357

Orakhelashvili A (2008) The interpretation of acts and rules in public international law. Oxford University Press, Oxford

Satzger H (2017) International and European criminal law, 2nd edn. C.H. Beck, München, Oxford, Baden-Baden

Simma B, Pulkowski D (2006) Of Planets and the universe: self-contained regimes in international law | Oxford Academic wwwsssxx. Eur J Int Law 17:483–529

Vranes E (2006) The definition of 'Norm Conflict' in international law and legal theory. Eur J Int Law 17:395–418. https://doi.org/10.1093/ejil/chl002

Chapter 7
The Regulation of Non-state Actors as Elements of the Domestic Penal Norms

Abstract Regulations formulated by non-state actors must be incorporated into the content of national penal norms, as derived by national courts. This chapter describes the method of such combined interpretation.

Keywords Penal norms · Element of norm · Non-state actors

At this point, let us turn to the presentation of the model of reasoning to be carried out by the national court in a situation where the legal basis for its decision will also consist of normative statements formulated by non-state actors. There are two considerations in favour of adopting the court's perspective.

Firstly, the court is the "end user" of the regulation. The actions of the executive and the legislature are only an intermediate stage here. Moreover, in view of the phenomenon of defragmentation of the law, it is the courts that are shifted the burden of implementation. It ceases to be a momentous act of a law-making character, but becomes commonplace—taking the form of peculiar interpretative procedures.[1] When deciding on criminal liability, a national court acts on the basis and within the limits of the law. It may not disregard any statement which it considers to be legally binding, nor take into account one which is not of that nature.[2]

Secondly, the content of the norm binding the court includes the content of the norm binding the individual. As indicated above, the condition for the attribution of criminal liability is a finding by the court/authority that the individual acted in violation of the law. The norm that binds the individual is here part of the standard of assessment used by the criminal court.

---

[1] Österdahl (2015, p. 127).

[2] Urueña (2015, p. 165).

D. Zając, *Non-state Actors Law-making and Domestic Criminal Law*,
SpringerBriefs in Law, https://doi.org/10.1007/978-3-031-47870-3_7

7.1 Non-state Actor Regulation as a Factor Affecting the Content of a Prohibition/Order Threatened with Punishment

The central element of the norm of the court (state actors) is the prohibition/order of a behaviour, the commission of which triggers the obligation to impose a penalty (see Sect. 3.1). The influence of regulations enacted by non-state actors on this element of the norm is significantly limited. The competence to formulate a prohibition/order is an element of *imperium*. It cannot be derived either from indications of knowledge or from the will of the addressee of the norm. Its source can only be a delegation. Establishing the content of a prohibition linked to the imposition of a penalty is therefore—at the current stage of development of international law—the domain of states (see Sect. 4.1, Fig. 7.1).

The content of the prohibition must be supplemented by the broader legal context. Here, four situations should be distinguished in which its content is clarified. In each of them, the court should consider the regulation, formulated by the non-state actor, as potential elements of the penal norm. Their function is to specify what exactly the prohibited (ordered) behaviour of the individual consists of (see Sect. 3.2, Fig. 7.2).

Firstly, it may be the case that a provision constituting a prohibition/order of a certain behaviour contains a reference to an act, issued by a non-state actor. For

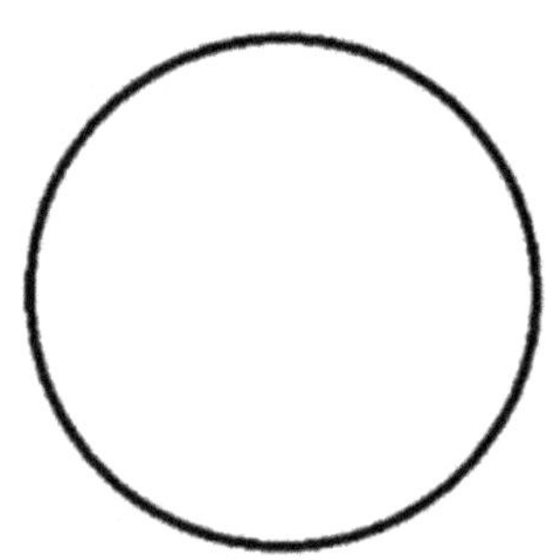

Fig. 7.1 Prohibition in basic form

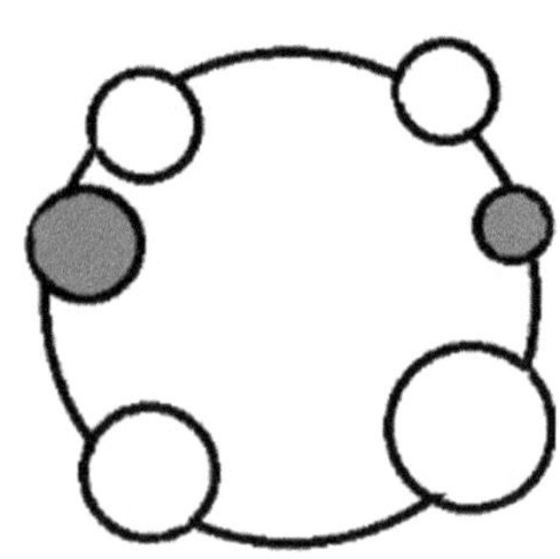

Fig. 7.2 Prohibition/order clarification process

example, § 38 WpHG (German Securities Trading Act—Wertpapierhandelsgesetz),[3] which refers to § 14 WpHG, prescribes the imposition of a penalty on a person who commits the communication of financial information in violation of the MAR Regulation. The scope of the penalisation—although determined by a decision of the German legislative authorities—in practice depends primarily on the current content of Union law. In situations where there is an express reference to a non-state actor regulation, the court does not in principle have the possibility to refuse to include it in the content of the penal norm. This would constitute an encroachment by the court on the competence of the legislature.

In the above situation the national legislator referred in the penal provision to a regulation enacted by a non-state actor (the EU), which was directly binding on the individual, at the time of its action (EU regulation with direct effect). However, a more problematic situation can be imagined. Suppose the legislator makes a reference to a non-state actor regulation which is not addressed to the individual (see Sect. 5.2). Can the court take into account a regulation of this type in the process of specifying the prohibition/order? It seems that the obligation to take it into account will only arise if the mere fact of a reference in the criminalising provision is considered a sufficient method of implementing such a regulation into the domestic legal system. Such a reference is legitimate as long as the content of the regulation to which the criminalising provision refers was identifiable at the time of the individual's action (e.g. it was duly promulgated). In this case, it will have obtained the knowledge of the scope of the criminalisation required to comply with the standard of *nullum crimen sine lege*. If the reference does not make it possible to determine the scope of criminalisation, the court should disregard the regulation, formulated by a non-state actor, about whose binding force there are doubts.

Secondly, the national legislator may use an open-ended reference based on the phrase: "unlawful" ("widerrechtlich").[4] Such a reference requires the establishment of a complete set of rules, binding upon the individual in the context of the alleged act. Such norms may include regulations formulated by non-state actors, provided that they are deemed to be binding on the individual at the time of the act or omission. In this case, the problem is not one of binding the reference, but of determining its actual scope. If it turns out that the individual's course of action was also determined by statements of non-state actors—it will be necessary to take them into account as elements of the norm.

---

[3] Gesetz über den Wertpapierhandel (Wertpapierhandelsgesetz - WpHG)-German Securities Trading Act, https://www.gesetze-im-internet.de/wphg/__38.html.

[4] For example, according to the § 123 of the German Criminal Code in the version published on 13 November 1998 (Federal Law Gazette I, p. 3322), as last amended by Article 2 of the Act of 22 November 2021, Federal Law Gazette I, p. 4906 (StGB), https://www.gesetze-im-internet.de/englisch_stgb/. Accessed 20 September 2023.: "(1) Whoever unlawfully enters the private premises, business premises or other enclosed property of another, or closed premises designated for public service or transportation, or whoever stays there without being authorised to do so and does not leave when requested to do so by the authorised person incurs a penalty of imprisonment for a term not exceeding one year or a fine".

Thirdly, even the absence of an express reference in the criminalising provision does not exclude the need to verify whether there has been a breach of the rules of conduct. Establishing liability for manslaughter due to improper construction techniques requires the determination of rules of art binding on the builder. The mere fact that a building has collapsed does not yet mean that there has been a breach of the rules of art, and it is only this circumstance that will make it possible to punish (see Sect. 3.1). These rules may be defined precisely by non-state actors. This is where ISO standards, rules of the game, formulated by sports federations, for example, will come into play. The invocation of regulations, binding on the moment of action, leads to a narrowing of the scope of the prohibition, which in its basic form is general and broad.

Fourthly, the legislator may use terms, the meaning of which must be established taking into account the statements formulated by non-state actors. There is no explicit order to take them into account in the process of determining the content of penal norms, but in a specific case it is their content that may be relevant in the interpretation process (see Sect. 4.3).

Fifth, non-state actor regulations may compel the state (court) to consider certain behaviour as permitted. For example, ECtHR jurisprudence has identified situations in which a restriction on the right of assembly is to be considered impermissible as contrary to the ECtHR.[5] The individual remains under the protection of this standard. If a national provision prescribes the criminalisation of unlawful assembly, the national court should, in the process of decoding the scope of illegality, take into account the provisions of the ECHR, as interpreted by the ECtHR. The mirror image of the above situation is the possibility of extending the criminal liability of a public official (see Sect. 4.2).

In order to illustrate the above with an example, let us analyse the impact of the ECHR judgment in Rabczewska v. Poland[6] on the interpretation of Article 196 of the Polish Criminal Code. As stated in the provision: "Whoever insults the religious feelings of others by publicly insulting an object of religious worship or a place intended for the public performance of religious rites, shall be subject to a fine, restriction of liberty or imprisonment of up to 2 years". The applicant was convicted on the basis of it, which she considered an unlawful interference with her right to

---

[5] Article 11 (1) of the European Convention for the Protection of Human Rights and Fundamental Freedoms, as amended by Protocols Nos. 11 and 14, 4 November 1950, ETS 5, https://www.echr.coe.int/documents/d/echr/convention_ENG. stipulates: "Everyone has the right to freedom of peaceful assembly and to freedom of association with others, including the right to form and to join trade unions for the protection of his interests". According ECtHR under its protection is for example: "Calling people through social networks to take part in an assembly"—see: Elvira Dmitriyeva v. Russia (nos. 60921/17 and 7202/18); Rainey et al. (2017, pp. 517–527).

[6] Rabczewska V. Poland, Request no 8257/13, ECtHR Judgment 15 September 2022, https://hudoc.echr.coe.int/app/conversion/docx/pdf?library=ECHR&id=001-219102&filename=CASE%20OF%20RABCZEWSKA%20v.%20POLAND.pdf&logEvent=False.

freedom of expression, precised in the Article 10 of the ECHR.[7] The ECtHR upheld the complaint, pointing out that: "The Court reiterates that a religious group must tolerate the denial by others of their religious beliefs and even the propagation by others of doctrines hostile to their faith, as long as the statements at issue do not incite to hatred or religious intolerance". As long as the statement constitutes a mere criticism of the cult's assumptions, also expressed in blunt terms, it remains protected by the standard protecting freedom of expression in Article 10 of the Convention.

In theory, the ECtHR judgment is only binding in the present case. In practice, it formulates an interpretation of Article 10 of the Convention, conducted in the context of the content of Article 196 of the Criminal Code, leading to its narrowing of the scope of criminalisation. Taking into account the ECtHR's statement, it should be said that the prohibition of behaviour that may violate religious feelings, derived from Article 196 of the Penal Code, applies only to such speech that constitutes incitement to hatred or religious intolerance.

As a result of the addition of the above elements to the content of the prohibition, it is narrowed down in such a way that it can serve as a benchmark for scrutinising an individual's behaviour for its illegality (see Sect. 7.5, Fig. 7.2).

7.2 Non-state Actor Regulation as a Factor Affecting the Other Conditions for the Attribution of Criminal Liability

A breach of a norm that binds an individual may or may not necessitate punishment. In addition to the violation of a prohibition, national criminal law systems also introduce a number of additional conditions for criminalisation: the requirement of age, of being of sound mind, of acting under conditions allowing fault to be attributed, etc. (see Sect. 3.2). These criteria do not impinge on the content of the individual's norm (Fig. 7.3). However, they are taken into account by the court as additional prerequisites for penal responsibility, co-constituting the court's norm (Sect. 7.5, Fig. 7.4). The formulation of criteria of this kind constitutes a form of exercise of *ius puniendi*. What takes place here is a distinction—at an abstract level—between punishable behaviour and behaviour that does not deserve punishment.

---

[7] European Convention for the Protection of Human Rights and Fundamental Freedoms, as amended by Protocols Nos. 11 and 14, 4 November 1950, ETS 5, https://www.echr.coe.int/documents/d/echr/convention_ENG. According to the Article 10: "1. Everyone has the right to freedom of expression. This right shall include freedom to hold opinions and to receive and impart information and ideas without interference by public authority and regardless of frontiers. This Article shall not prevent States from requiring the licensing of broadcasting, television or cinema enterprises. 2. The exercise of these freedoms, since it carries with it duties and responsibilities, may be subject to such formalities, conditions, restrictions or penalties as are prescribed by law and are necessary in a democratic society, in the interests of national security, territorial integrity or public safety, for the prevention of disorder or crime, for the protection of health or morals, for the protection of the reputation or rights of others, for preventing the disclosure of information received in confidence, or for maintaining the authority and impartiality of the judiciary".

Fig. 7.3 Norm of the individual in its final form

Fig. 7.4 Hypothesis of the norm of the court

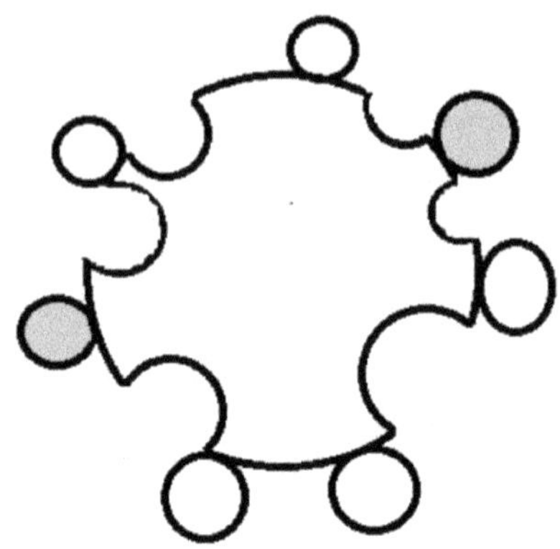

In order to determine the potential impact of the regulation of non-state actors on the shape of this element of the penal norm, two aspects of potential impact must be distinguished. Firstly, non-state actor regulation may lead to an expansion of criminalisation in relation to the content of domestic law, and secondly, it may have the effect of narrowing it.

In the first case, the non-state actor must act on the basis of and within the competence to establish the criteria for criminalisation, within the meaning of the principle of *nullum crimen sine lege*. This is because there is an expansion of the scope of criminalisation. In practice, regulations of this type are not formulated by non-state actors at the current stage of development of international law. However, if they are established, on the basis and within the limits of its competence, the court will have limited possibilities to refuse to take them into account (see Sect. 4.1).

Secondly, the regulation of a non-state actor may have a limiting function of ius puniendi, prohibiting in certain cases the attribution of criminal liability. As already indicated, there is no interference with the nullum crimen standard here—as it always works in favour of the individual. This type of regulation is also rare. At the level of international law, for example, there is no order to respect necessary defence as a circumstance precluding punishment.[8] However, it is theoretically conceivable that

[8] Prevention of human rights violations committed with small arms and light weapons Final report submitted by Barbara Frey, Special Rapporteur, in accordance with Sub-Commission resolution 2002/25, p. 9; Klip (2021, p. 280).

Fig. 7.5 An order to impose a penalty within the statutory limits—in basic form

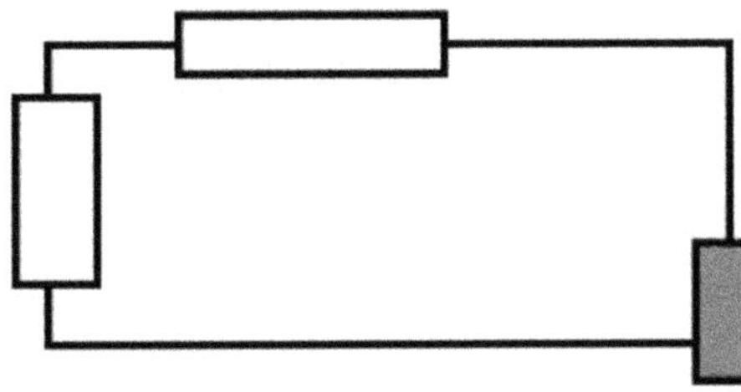

Fig. 7.6 The limits of the penalty clarification process

a non-state actor would supplement, for example, the principle of fault in a binding manner with such elements that were not known at the national level.[9]

7.3 Non-state Actor Regulation as a Factor Affecting Limits of Penalties

The last element of the norm is a disposition addressed to the court and ordering it to impose a punishment on an individual. It consists of the statutory threat of punishment, usually specified in the typifying provision (see Sect. 7.5, Fig. 7.5), and additional criteria that modify the shape of these limits (see Sect. 7.5, Fig. 7.6). Both the statutory threat limits and the additional penalty criteria are the result of a relatively free decision of the states. In practice, there are no statements formulated by non-state actors that indicate what punishment should be imposed on an individual. Positive regulation is lacking here.

By contrast, non-state actors' regulations may set limits to forms of repression in those areas where punishment may violate human rights. Such impact is of a specific nature, due to the shape of the disposition of the norm binding on the court. In fact, the order to impose punishment takes the form of a description of the statutory limits of its measure, contained in the penalising provision. The generally outlined limits are then further specified by a series of regulations, usually contained in the general part of criminal law (sentencing directives). Absolute exceptions include those situations, where it has been determined at the statutory level what specific penalty should be

[9] Panebianco (2015, p. 55).

imposed on the offender.[10] As a general rule, the national court will therefore have the possibility to “modify” the sentencing limits—within its discretion. It will simply refrain from imposing a penalty that is contrary to the non-state actor regulation. Where the sentencing limits are set too narrowly for such a modification to occur, there will be a conflict of normative statements (see Sect. 6.4).

An example of this type of statement can be found in the judgment of the ECtHR, declaring a sentence of life imprisonment without the possibility of applying for conditional early release to be contrary to Article 3 of the ECHR.[11] If the national legislator does not provide for the possibility of seeking a reduction of the sentence at the enforcement stage, the statutory limits of the sentence at the judicial stage should be modified accordingly. The court, acting within the limits of its powers, should in this situation take into account the possibility of conditional release already in the judgment itself or impose a different type of sentence.

7.4 The Final Shape of the Court’s Norm

The manner of the court’s inference characterised above, interpreting the norm using regulations formulated by a non-state actor, can be illustrated graphically.

First of all, the court should identify the provision, which constitutes a prohibition/order of conduct. At present, its source will be either national or—theoretically—EU law. Graphically, this can be shown as a circle.

The general prohibition/order is then fleshed out with regulations specifying the desired course of action for the individual, formulated both at national (white dots)

---

[10] For example, according to § 211 (1) of the German Criminal Code in the version published on 13 November 1998 (Federal Law Gazette I, p. 3322), as last amended by Article 2 of the Act of 22 November 2021, Federal Law Gazette I, p. 4906 (StGB), https://www.gesetze-im-internet.de/englisch_stgb/. Accessed 20 September 2023: (1) “Whoever commits murder under the conditions of this provision incurs a penalty of imprisonment for life”. In accordance with the judiciary of the German Federal Constitutional Court (Bundesverfassungsgericht, judgmenet BVerfG, 21.06.1977–1 BvL 14/76): “Life imprisonment is constitutional if the sentenced person (beyond the prospect of pardon) retains the possibility of a suspended sentence” (own translation, original phrase: “lebenslange Freiheitsstrafe ist verfassungsmäßig, wenn dem Verurteilten (über die Aussicht auf Begnadigung hinaus) die Möglichkeit einer Strafaussetzung verbleibt”).

[11] Vinter and Others v. the United Kingdom [GC]—66069/09, 130/10 and 3896/10, Judgment 9.7.2013 [GC], https://hudoc.echr.coe.int/app/conversion/pdf/?library=ECHR&id=002-7652&filename=002-7652.pdf. The regulations formulated in this respect may also be less categorical in nature. For example, in Committee of Ministers of Council (Council of Europe) Resolution (76) on The Treatment of Long-Term Prisoners, Adopted By The Committee Of Ministers On 17 February 1976, https://rm.coe.int/16804f2385, indicated that it is necessary to: “grant the prisoner conditional release, subject to the statutory requirements relating to time served, as soon as a favourable prognosis can be formulated; considerations of general prevention alone should not justify refusal of conditional release”, and recommended: “adapt to life sentences the same principles as apply to long-term sentences”. The Explanatory Memorandum accompanying Council of Europe Recommendation No. 2003(22) explicitly indicates that persons sentenced to life imprisonment should also not be deprived of the hope of conditional release—https://rm.coe.int/16800ccb5d.

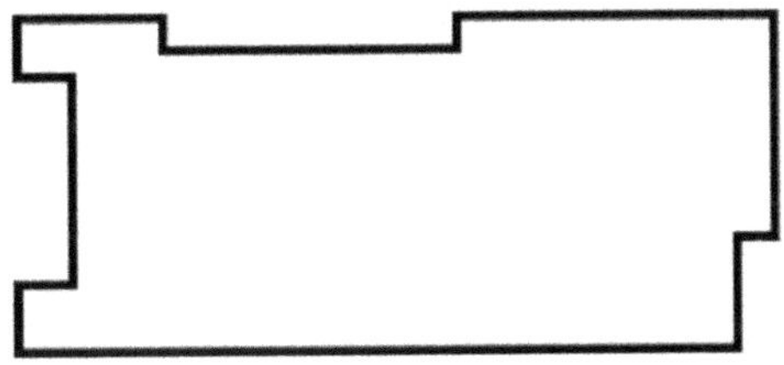

Fig. 7.7 Disposition of the norm of the court

and international levels (grey dots). This is where the impact of the legislative activity of non-state actors is most clearly visible.

This establishes a norm of individual that is binding in a given case. It is narrower than the prohibition in its original form.

If the offender's behaviour is deemed to be contrary to the norm that binds him (it fits inside the circle thus carved out), the court should proceed to verify the subsequent criteria for the attribution of penal norms. These are broader than the mere violation of the norm. At this stage, non-state actors may formulate additional criteria—in practice narrowing the scope of criminalisation (see Sect. 5.2 and the grey field). In this way, the hypothesis of the norm binding on the authority will be established.

If it is acknowledged that all the prerequisites contained in the hypothesis of the norm of the court have been fulfilled, it is necessary to proceed to determining the content of its disposition. The starting point should be the penalising provision containing the description of the limits of the statutory threat of punishment.

However, the statutory limits contained in the provision are subject to modifications—on the part of national laws and international regulations. In this respect, too, there is a fine-tuning. In practice, it may happen that the statements of non-state actors affect the shape of the potential repression in a certain way, reducing its severity (grey field).

As a result of the above, the content of the disposition of the norm that is binding on the court is established. It constitutes the area in which the court navigates when making its decision on the level of punishment.

The compilation of all stages illustrates the entire exegesis process. If the court is of the view that all the prerequisites of the norm's hypothesis have been met, it should impose a punishment within the limits of its disposition.

If Fig. 7.4 is met then the court must respond in a way that remains within the limits of the Fig. 7.7.

References

Klip A (2021) European criminal law: an integrative approach, 4th edn. Intersentia, Cambridge Antwerp Chicago

Österdahl I (2015) (International) Law! In: Liivoja R, Petman J (eds) International law-making: essays in honour of Jan Klabbers, 1st edn. Routledge, Abingdon, Oxon

Panebianco G (2015) The Nulla Poena Sine Culpa principle in European courts case law. In: Ruggeri S (ed) Human rights in European criminal law: new developments in European legislation and case law after the Lisbon treaty, 2015th edn. Springer, New York, NY

Rainey B, Wicks E, Ovey C (2017) The European convention on human rights, 7th edn. Oxford University Press, New York, NY

Urueña R (2015) Law-making through comparative international law? In: Liivoja R, Petman J (eds) International law-making: essays in honour of Jan Klabbers, 1st edn. Routledge, Abingdon, Oxon

Chapter 8
Conclusions

Regulations of non-state actors can affect any element of the penal norms and have a real impact on the shape of an individual's criminal responsibility. A national court is obliged to take such provisions into account when interpreting penal norms, if it considers that they may form part of the norm. This is not a discretionary decision on the part of the court, but a necessity arising from the fact that the court is bound by the law in its decision-making.

The extent and nature of this influence is not uniform. It depends mainly on two factors.

First, the source of the non-state actor's authority in the field of law-making is crucial. For the purposes of this study, a distinction is made between delegation of competences, consent and transfer of knowledge. Delegation is the strongest basis for formulating statements of authoritative power. Such statements derive their force from the original will of the state, even though they are formally issued by a non-state actor. Consent and transfer of knowledge are considered weaker sources. The rules formulated on the basis of them do not belong to the sphere of the empire—their influence on the form of criminal liability is indirect. In a given situation, however, it may turn out that a binding rule based on consent is of decisive importance in determining whether a certain conduct was prohibited.

Second, the extent and nature of the influence of the statements of a non-state actor on the shape of criminal liability of individual is determined by the content of the regulation. Every rule must specify its content and, at least indirectly, its addressee. If the statement is addressed to the state, it cannot directly bind the individual by shaping his or her behaviour. It can, however, limit the scope of criminalisation, restrict the freedom of the state and extend the scope of civil liberties. This is how, for example, human rights work.

Such influence varies in intensity in relation to the different elements of criminal law. The strongest impact can be observed in the case of the criteria specifying/narrowing the content of the prohibition/order. This element has a more discursive character and its content can be modified to a certain extent on the basis of the

D. Zając, *Non-state Actors Law-making and Domestic Criminal Law*,
SpringerBriefs in Law, https://doi.org/10.1007/978-3-031-47870-3_8

consent or knowledge of the individual. Very rarely does a statement by a non-state actor constitute a "pure" prohibition. In fact, it never specifies an order to impose a specific punishment.

Despite this significant influence of non-state actor statements on the shape of criminal responsibility, it is to a large extent unconscious. On the one hand, non-state actors do not explicitly seek to shape criminal norms in a particular way, but only to define a certain desirable standard of behaviour. On the other hand, state authorities like to refer to statements of non-state actors in the process of decoding norms. This gives them the *de facto* value of commonly binding law. The courts play a key role in this process. It is their task to provide justice on the basis of and within the limits of the law. The judicial power therefore also includes the duty to review normative statements for their binding force. It is the court that ultimately decides which statements to include in the content of the norm. In the absence of the mandatory binding character of norms formulated by non-state actors, the pronouncement of the national court is of tremendous importance here.

This process must take place within the framework of structured reasoning. In this way, the authorities will be able to ensure the consistency of the solutions applied and avoid arbitrariness. It has been the aim of the author of these words to present such reasoning in an exemplary manner. If the reader has found in this book an indication of how to incorporate the normative statements of non-state actors into the content of the norms interpreted for the purposes of a particular adjudication, then this objective has been achieved.

GPSR Compliance
The European Union's (EU) General Product Safety Regulation (GPSR) is a set of rules that requires consumer products to be safe and our obligations to ensure this.

If you have any concerns about our products, you can contact us on

ProductSafety@springernature.com

In case Publisher is established outside the EU, the EU authorized representative is:

Springer Nature Customer Service Center GmbH
Europaplatz 3
69115 Heidelberg, Germany

www.ingramcontent.com/pod-product-compliance
Ingram Content Group UK Ltd.
Pitfield, Milton Keynes, MK11 3LW, UK
UKHW020151290926
15471UKWH00004B/817
* 9 7 8 3 0 3 1 4 7 8 6 9 7 *